GRAPHIC DESIGN
IN THE COMPUTER AGE
General Editor: André Jute

ILLUSTRATION
for professional communicators
Vicky Squires

Batsford

Contents

Note: Words in **bold** throughout are explained further in the glossary on pp 91-94

Acknowledgements

All illustrations are by Vicky Squires exclusively in *Aldus Freehand*. All text was written in *Microsoft Word* and pages designed in *Quark Xpress*. Many thanks to the **National Extension College, Cornhill Publications** and **Human Computer Interface** for kind permission to reproduce illustrations commissioned by them.

Text and illustrations © 1993 by Vicky Squires.

Driving Standards Agency illustrations are Crown copyright and are reproduced with the permission of the Controller of HMSO.

The right of Vicky Squires to be identified as the author and illustrator of this work has been asserted by her in accordance with the Copyright, Designs and Patents Act 1988.

A CIP catalogue record for this book is available from the British Library.

ISBN 0 7134 7171 9

Jacket design: André Jute
Interior design: Vicky Squires
Typeset and originated by The Bureau, B.P. Integraphics, Bath
Printed in Singapore for the publishers
B. T. Batsford Ltd
4 Fitzhardinge Street
London W1H 0AH

Graphic Design in the Computer Age
General Editor: André Jute

The blank sheet

The day has arrived! After volunteering your services as an illustrator to family, friends, local volunteer groups, publishing houses or vast business corporations, you have received your first commission. Here you sit with rough notes, typed brief or something similar in one hand and a blank sheet of paper in the other. Where do you start?

It is easy to take fright at this point, as your options seem limitless, but there are a number of questions to be answered before you can put mouse to mat or pencil to paper.

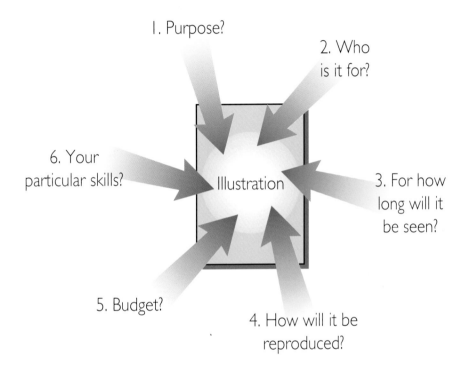

An illustration – like any other product – can accurately be judged on how well it fits its purpose. Questions 1, 2 and 3 (with the blue arrows) are really about this; this is the intellectual part of equation. Questions 4, 5 and 6 (with the brown arrows) are the practical considerations.

Once you have answers to all these questions, you will be ready to start, and that computer screen or blank sheet of paper will not seem so daunting.

What is the purpose of your illustration?

Decorative or instructional?

Illustrations can range in purpose from the wholly decorative to those which can stand alone and convey a message without the addition of words. The following diagram is intended to show a breakdown of the various types of illustration work – the main point being that purely decorative work is a very small proportion of the whole.

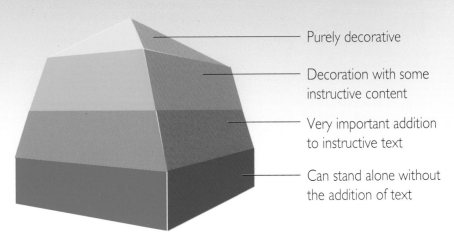

Purely decorative

Decoration with some instructive content

Very important addition to instructive text

Can stand alone without the addition of text

Purely decorative

This is the end of the illustration spectrum which offers the most artistic freedom. It's illustration for its own sake; the text can be understood perfectly well without it.

From 'Coming into Hospital'. An information booklet in nine languages for patients with little English. The illustrations add little to the understanding, but help make the publication more approachable.

Decorative, with some instructive content

Charts and diagrams for newspapers, illustrations of products for magazines, food items for cookery books are examples of the type of image that fall into this category. 'Can you do something exciting with this chart? There are hardly any pics in this article' is usually the kind of introduction you get to this type of work. It usually involves working at great speed with very few constraints, and can be very stimulating.

Figures were suppled for this 'filler' diagram for Marketing Director International,Cornhill Publications.

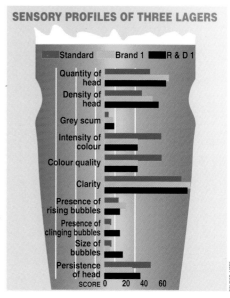

When tackling such a job, it is best to start with a brainstorming session; quickly jot down any visual images that come to mind. Then see what you have available in the way of reference or existing images. A computer has a great advantage over traditional methods here, as you can snatch previously-generated images, modify them by changing colour, line-thickness and so on, and drop them into your new chart.

Here again, figures were supplied in the form of a bar chart. With only three bars, it had little visual interest. A world map stored on the computer from previous work made a good background, and yet the whole diagram took very little time. From Global Investment Management, Cornhill Publications.

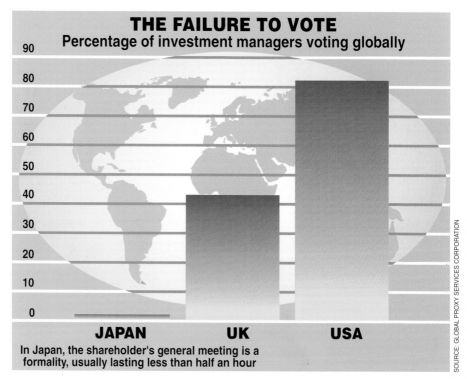

A very important addition to an instructive text

The text contains all the information required, but a picture is essential to describe a difficult action or manoeuvre. Illustration is often preferred to photography for this kind of use. Whereas a photograph would include everything in detail, an illustration need only include the details in question; other areas can be simplified, or left out entirely. There are no pedestrians, litter, cyclists and so on in this street as there doubtless would have been in a photograph of a similar scene. We don't want to distract attention from the main point of this picture, which is the action of the motor vehicles.

It's also possible to choose an odd angle of perspective. Viewed from street level, it would have been difficult to show these manoeuvres, but a bird's-eye view adds a great deal of clarity.

From The Driving Manual (HMSO/DSA).

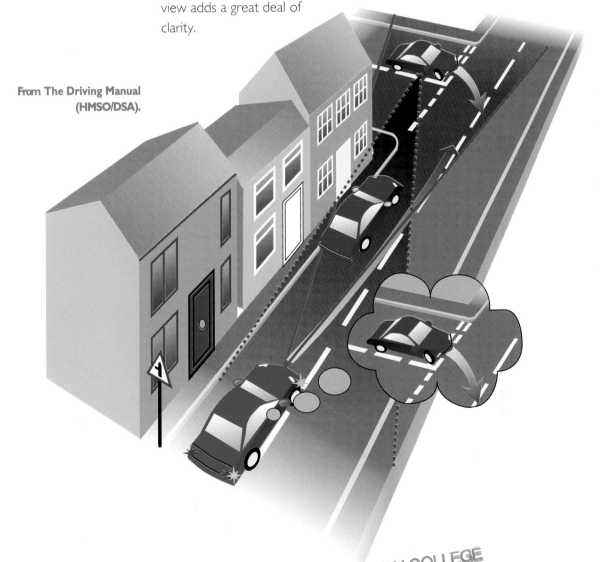

1 What is the purpose of your illustration?

Illustrations that can stand alone without text

This commands the most accuracy and attention to detail. This is the kind of work you find in instruction manuals for electrical appliances, cars, toys and so on. These must be easily understood by a very wide range of people; some may have reading problems, for example, whereas others may not even speak the language of the document.

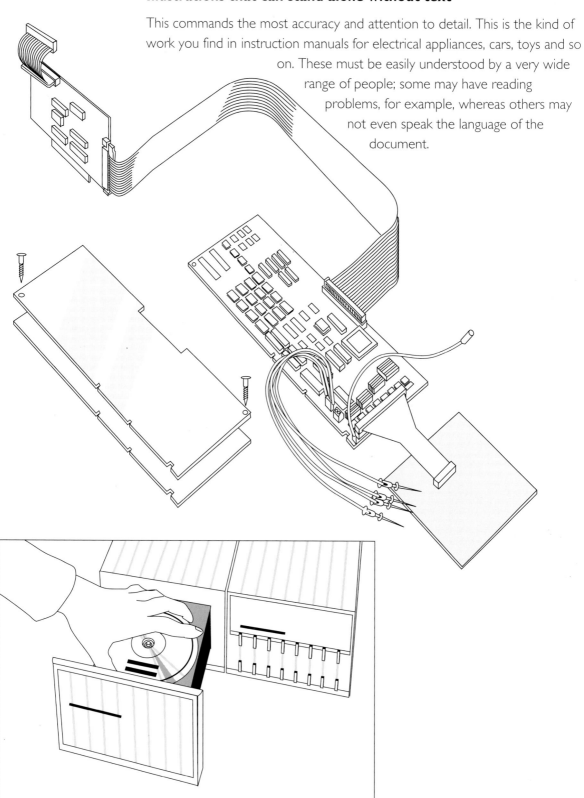

What is the client trying to say?

By 'client' I mean the person who gave you the brief; this can be a commissioning editor, art director, publicity manager of a large industry, producer of your local amateur dramatic society's latest venture … the list is endless, and part of the pleasure of the job is the people you meet.

This person will usually have a very clear idea of what they want the image to be. (In my experience it is very rare to be casually tossed a manuscript and told to illustrate whatever aspects you like.) It is very important that you understand the brief accurately, and advisable to spend plenty of time at your meeting clarifying every aspect. Written descriptions can range from 'cartoon here' circled in the manuscript, right up to a very detailed and accurate drawing that just needs a neat reworking. Take plenty of notes yourself if they are not supplied. Make sure that you are well briefed.

Full colour illustration for the **Council for Physical Recreation's** *leaflet* **'Play Safe with Water Sport.'**

The main thing to remember is that your answer lies in the brief. You can produce a magnificent piece of work, but if it does not convey the message the client wants, it will be useless.

At this point I should mention it is wise to cultivate a thick skin if you fancy a full time career in illustration. From time to time you will have to face the fact that, although perfectly accurate and adhering to the brief, your work may be rejected because the client just doesn't like it. Don't waste too much time grieving and losing your confidence – this happens to all illustrators, even the most famous!

Who is it for?

Old? Young?

What is your likely audience? Is your work intended for a serious, mature student, studying in the evening, or is it for young children learning to read? You can see that the style would be quite dramatically different, the mature student needing a very complex, accurate, labelled drawing and the child a more colourful, simple image. This is a very obvious example of course, but it is the type of decision you have to make for every piece of work. The main question to be answered is 'why are they looking at this?' Do they really need clear information, or is it just a lively picture to jolly the words along?

The top row of illustrations is from an instruction leaflet for a 'sit and ride' wooden plane (Philco Toys), which comes in easy-to-assemble pieces. There were twelve pictures altogether; these three deal with the assembly of the child's seat and tail section.

The second row of illustrations is an imaginary interpretation of the same set of instructions.

Relaxed? Under pressure?

What mood is the reader likely to be in? Is this a colour illustration for a magazine, for example, when your audience is likely to be comfortable and relaxed? Or is it a set of instructions to assemble a toy? You can imagine the scene – Christmas morning, children and toys everywhere, and someone struggling with the following examples:

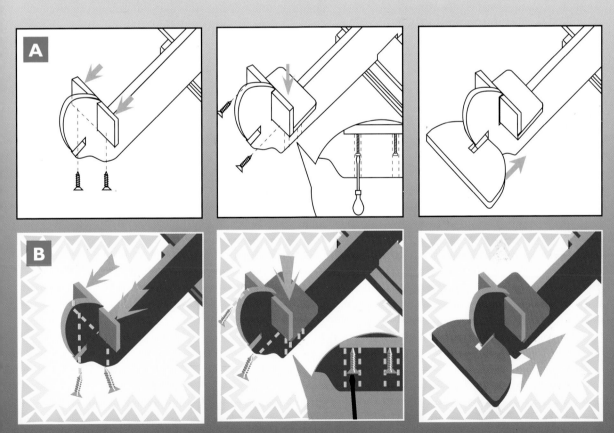

Which set do think is more appropriate for the mood and needs of your audience? The three diagrams in example **A** are clean, restrained and lacking in superfluous detail. They convey the sequence of assembly clearly. **B** shows a much more self-indulgent treatment. The odd shapes of the arrows and jazzy background pattern all serve to distract us from the main points. Although lively and attractive, in this context they would be irritating and difficult to understand.

From 'Coming into Hospital'. This was printed in nine languages – Arabic, Bengali, Chinese, Greek, Gujarati, Punjabi, Turkish, Urdu and Vietnamese – so it was an obvious decision to portray these nationalities in the pictures.

From **The Driving Manual (HMSO/DSA).** *This is aimed at anybody wishing to improve their driving skills – a very wide audience. This small picture shows a variety of ages, genders and racial types.*

Race? Gender?

If you are illustrating a large number of people, either in one illustration, or in a series running throughout a publication, it is essential to include a good mixture of male/female and different racial types. You don't want any particular section of society to feel alienated in any way by your illustration. The only exception to this would be an item aimed at a specific group – health information written in Hindu, for example – where obviously you would make all the people in your illustration Asian.

Perhaps you can include a handicapped person in your illustration? If you have a café scene, for example, why not have one of the people in a wheelchair? Handicapped people so rarely feature in illustration, it's easy to see why they claim to be invisible.

Sexual stereotyping

This requires very sensitive handling. If you are in a position where you are showing a number of different professions – say, a French language school textbook – it would be good to make 'le docteur' (for example) female. Perhaps you are able to show an office scene where the boss is female, for a change. It really needs a delicate hand and common sense; you can't rush through your French textbook making everybody female, including the coal-face worker and the local gendarme! There is obviously a point at which it becomes ridiculous and begins to detract from the true function of the publication.

Two illustrations from **The Motorcycling Manual (HMSO/DSA).**

The illustrations below came from a publication on motorcycling. There was a mixture of male and female motorcyclists. However, had there been the opportunity to show only *one* motorcyclist, it would have been best to show a male – after all, female motorcyclists are very much in the minority.

For how long will it be seen?

What is the shelf-life of your illustration? A school textbook, for instance, could be printed and reprinted many times over a decade or more; copies of your illustration could still be in existence fifteen or twenty years from now. At the other extreme, an illustration you did for last week's Sunday news magazine will be in the trash can in a few days.

These factors should influence your choice of style. A highly quirky or eccentric style is unsuitable for an encyclopaedia or manual because it will soon look dated, but it will be just the thing for a rock concert poster, which will be around for a short time.

*From **The Driving Manual (HMSO/DSA)**. This was difficult; the manual this was replacing had been in print for nearly twenty years, and we had to assume this would have the same sort of lifespan. However, motor vehicles are notorious for changing style. I've opted for a realistic representation, and made the car anonymous but as modern and aerodynamic as possible.*

Fashion

The main problem with fashion, be it in illustration, clothes, or music, is that it is usually followed by a rebound period when that same fashion can seem tedious and sometimes even ridiculous. A novel illustration style appears, and before long it is widely copied. The market is flooded with it, and everywhere we look we see examples – sometimes well-executed, sometimes not. Before long, boredom sets in and the style is rejected. This is unfortunate for you if it's the only style in your repertoire!

GAMES & SPORTS

Go ahead and cultivate your highly eccentric style by all means. With a bit of luck it will become 'flavour of the month', and for a year or two you will be inundated with work, and copied by everybody. Make the most of it, but don't expect it to last forever, and do brace yourself for the 'Oh, not that old style again…' backlash that may follow the success. Cultivate some more styles so that you don't find yourself suddenly redundant as fashion moves on.

These sportsmen illustrated a leaflet for the **Central Council of Physical Recreation.** *This is reprinted every year or two, so I felt safe giving it a free and quirky treatment.*

A 'woodcut' style for an advertising leaflet for Down Hall, a high class hotel. Here again, it was likely to have a lifespan of only a year or so, at which point it would probably be redesigned, and I felt able to approach it quite freely.

(This is one of a series of illustrations in the leaflet. I discuss the whole series in greater detail on pp 60-65 of this book)

How will it be reproduced?

There are many ways of reproducing an illustration, ranging from a black and white photocopy or laser print, right the way up through two-, three-, four- and more colour printing. An excellent result can be achieved throughout the whole range, but it's essential to have a good understanding of what is possible in each case.

Black and white illustration

'Single colour' would perhaps be a more accurate title for this, as it can be printed in any one colour, but in practice it is mostly black and white.

The most important point to be remembered throughout is that the illustration you create will, at some point, have to be reproduced by the use of inked areas on a metal or rubber **plate**, or a **silk-screen**. (This is also true of colour illustration, which we will be dealing with later.) A black and white photograph is an example of **continuous tone**; this is the effect of light on a sensitized paper, and countless shades of grey can be created. This differs profoundly from all printing techniques, which are the application of solid areas of ink onto a surface. The image is created by the presence or absence of ink on that surface. Shades of grey are produced by breaking the image into a pattern, usually dots or lines, which is called a **half-tone screen.** This gives the illusion of grey, but when viewed through a magnifying glass the pattern of solid areas can be seen. The illusion of shades of grey can also be created by hand, using, for example, cross-hatching or dots.

The dots in a half-tone vary in frequency.

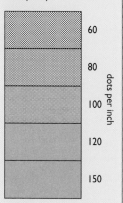

	60
	80
	100
	120
	150

dots per inch

60 lines per inch gives a coarse tint, suitable for printing on paper with a rough surface (such as newsprint).

150 lines per inch gives a very fine tint which needs a smooth-surfaced paper to reproduce well.

The dots also vary in size, to create different shades of grey.

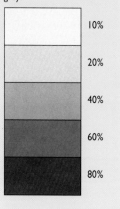

	10%
	20%
	40%
	60%
	80%

This illustration was printed on a manila envelope, hence the bold approach.

This all sounds quite obvious, but it is surprising how often illustrations are impaired by the illustrator failing to grasp this basic fact. If you have been commissioned to do a 'black and white line illustration', then a pen-and-ink drawing with a selection of subtle grey washes will not meet the requirements. The grey areas, if they are to reproduce at all, will have to be half-toned by being photographed through a screen, which may be far in excess of your client's budget. The end result may disappoint *you*, too, because the technique of half-toning will put small white dots in all your black lines, and reduce the contrast. Pencil sketches can be disappointing as well; they will be coarser when half-toned, and will lose the continuous-tone effect which is part of their charm. This doesn't mean that all these attractive, loose techniques have to be abandoned, but you must remember that the finished result is a pattern of solid, inked areas (however small these may be, in the case of a fine tone). Perhaps you can create a loose tone on your pen drawing by using a textured paper and lightly rubbing a black crayon over the tonal areas? This will break it up into dots which can be picked up by the printer's camera.

There are also many rub-on tones and textures available in art and graphic shops which reproduce well.

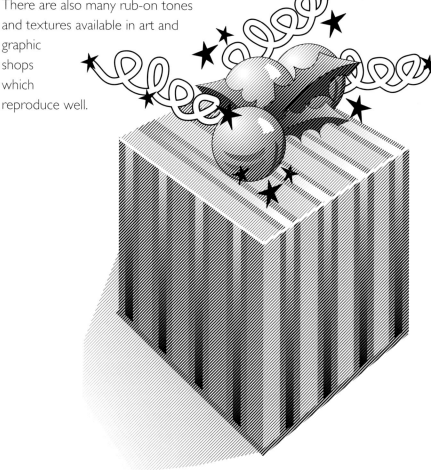

Photocopies and laser prints

In the past it was impossible to achieve a large area of good, solid black on a photocopy. Now the results are so good they can be indistinguishable from black and white printing. If you are commissioned to do work which will be reproduced this way, don't regard it as a downmarket job, unworthy of much attention. Posters for local amateur dramatic productions and newsletters for various voluntary groups are examples of this type of work, and although not particularly lucrative, they are often the projects which offer the most excitement and creative freedom. If you are in the early stages of your illustration career, they have the added advantage of getting your work to a wide audience, possibly new potential customers, so do make sure that your name appears discreetly on them. (It often seems that the larger the signature, the worse the work of art – so discretion is the key!)

Bold lines and coarse tints are used on this picture, which was specifically designed to be photocopied.

Laser prints from computers fall into the same category as photocopies, requiring strong, bold images. There is also a large and increasing market for the use of laser prints as camera-ready artwork for certain types of publication. Specialist teaching materials and manuals for industrial equipment, where perhaps only 500 or 1000 copies are needed, fall into this category. A well-designed, boldly illustrated laser-printed document is perfect for this use. Here we have a case of new technology creating a new market – this type of document would probably have just been neatly typewritten in the past.

Technical tips

The computer can provide many different tints and patterns - don't just limit yourself to using the default half-tone screen.

Try lines at different frequencies…   and different angles.   Try a round dot…   or patterned fills.

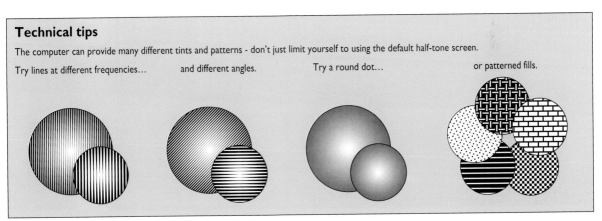

Newspapers

Newspapers represent the greatest challenge for black and white illustration. In this discipline you run the gauntlet of everything that modern printing techniques can throw at you! Your illustration can be under-inked, over-inked, reduced, cut up, and sometimes even pasted in upside down. It has to be strong enough to stand out on a crowded page where everything is literally screaming for attention. The off-white newsprint reduces contrast, so the crisp black and white bromide that you supplied to the newspaper can look disappointingly flat when you see it in print a few days later.

Start by researching the newspaper, and the area of that newspaper, in which your picture is going to appear. Perhaps you are drawing an electrician at work for an advertisement in the 'local services' column; are the neighbouring advertisements predominantly light or dark? If light, perhaps you could put your electrician in a dark overall so that your picture will stand out by contrast. Do make sure it's bold; don't use lines less than 0.4 mm wide, and don't use a screen finer than 60 lines per inch. In fact, if you want to create grey, perhaps it would be best to use lines or patterns. Do prepare yourself to find the printed result rather lifeless, and do congratulate yourself if, having gone through all this, your illustration looks quite good!

A bold set of conservatories used in a newspaper advertisement for a double glazing company.

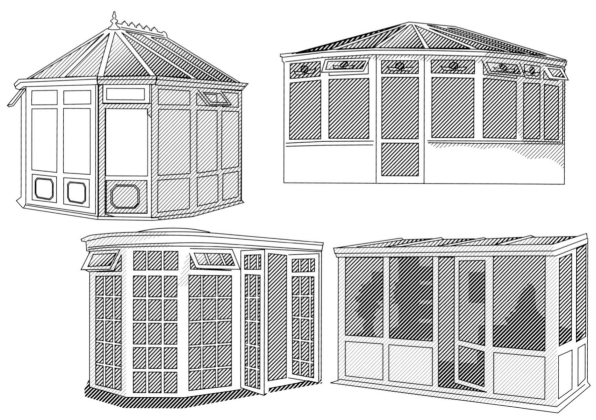

Black and white in quality publications

Not all black and white illustration is low budget and printed on poor quality paper. Cookery books, encyclopedias and do-it-yourself manuals are all examples where black and white illustrations may be printed on high quality, smooth paper. Here, you can use fine lines (0.1 mm wide) and tints of 150 or more lines per inch.

Printing in more than one colour

To print each colour requires the press to be inked up in that colour, and the paper to be passed through once. This sometimes causes confusion; two-colour work passes through the press *twice*, three-colour work is passed through the press *three* times. One of the 'colours' referred to in these cases is probably black, or may even be a special varnish with no colour at all. It would be more accurate to call two-colour printing 'two-*pass* printing', because the number actually refers to the number of *passes* through the press. Clients will often ask for a job in 'two-colour' when what they actually have in mind is something printed in black on a coloured paper – only a single pass, and therefore properly called printing in one colour. On the other hand, the client may not be regarding black as a colour at all, and be thinking of two *extra* colours – i.e. three-colour printing! Do make sure when you get the brief that both you and the client are absolutely clear on these points.

In illustrations using more than one colour, the areas to be printed in the different colours need to be separated in some way.

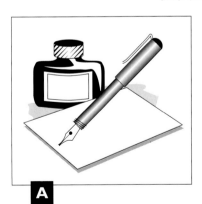
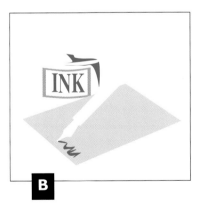

A shows what is printed by the black plate, **B** shows what is printed by the blue plate, and **C** shows the finished result.

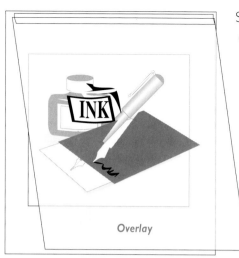

Overlay

Illustration on board

Separation was traditionally done by producing an illustration (in black) on board and putting an overlay on top, on which the areas of second colour could be indicated (again in black). This would then be photographed by the printer and converted to the positive or negative film separations needed to transfer the image to the printing plate.

The computer, however, allows the work to be shown to the client in the form of laser prints. The client can then make suggestions and alterations until it meets with his or her total approval. At this point it can be run out directly from the computer as final film separations. This not only saves time and money, but improves accuracy. With the traditional method, there are margins of error at each stage. For example, the illustrator may not produce a tightly-registered overlay, and this could be further exacerbated by the camera-work of the printer whose camera may have a slight fault in the lens or lighting. The computer output is a true, first generation of the artwork, and in printing, the first generation always gives the most crisp results.

The use of the computer has blurred the edges of the various printing crafts. In the past, the illustrator could leave the choice of half-tone dot size, for example, to the printer. Now this falls into the artist's realm of responsibility, hence the need for a more in-depth knowledge of printing techniques. This is very challenging, but ultimately worthwhile as it gives the illustrator more control over the finished, printed result. Let's examine each of the various multiple-colour options – two-, three-, four- and more colour – in turn.

Two-colour printing

This is frequently used, and can be extremely effective. Posters and book covers are often printed in two colours.

In the past it was often difficult to convey to a printer exactly what colours you had chosen for your image; in fact, it was probably one of the biggest areas of poor communication and the ultimate disappointment for both illustrator and client. Thankfully, printing inks have become standardised over the years, and at present the **Pantone Matching System** is commonly used. Coloured inks are encoded with numbers, which are used universally; if you specify **PMS123** in one country it will be matched perfectly by a printer thousands of miles away. The same numbering system is not limited to printing inks; you can purchase coloured papers, inks, felt-tipped pens and so on, all coded in the same way.

Here are a few four-colour representations of **Pantone** colours and their numbers. To show the true Pantone inks would involve a separate pass through the press for each – 14 extra printings in this case! This is why a Pantone swatch book, with samples of the whole range, is so expensive; each colour being mixed and printed separately. It's nevertheless a sound investment to obtain one as soon as possible in your illustration career.

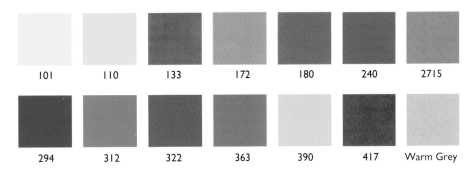

| 101 | 110 | 133 | 172 | 180 | 240 | 2715 |

| 294 | 312 | 322 | 363 | 390 | 417 | Warm Grey |

Don't forget that tints can also be applied of any colour you use. On the left are representations of a few tints in *PMS 172*.

| 100% (sometimes described as 'solid') |

| 80% |

| 60% |

| 40% |

| 20% |

The most predictable results in two-colour work can be obtained by choosing black as your second colour. It will overprint whatever colour you choose densely, and give maximum definition to your lines. Don't forget to use the full range of tints, both of black and of the colour, to get the most out of your two colours.

A

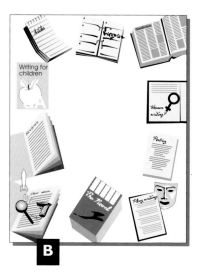

B

C

On the two-colour book cover shown here, **A** shows what is printed by the green plate, **B** shows the black plate, and **C** the finished printed result, a composite of the two. This information was given to the printer in the form of **positive film separations**, one for the black and one for the green areas. Note the use of tints of both black and green to give an added richness to the illustrations.

Another rather more daring technique is to use two colours which can overprint each other to produce a third; yellow and blue to produce green, or yellow and red to produce orange, for example. The most commonly used printing inks are transparent and can be successfully overlaid this way. The main drawback of this technique is that you lose the definition which black always achieves. Secondly, it can be a bit of a hit-and-miss technique choosing two colours which produce an attractive, contrasting, third colour. Colour swatch books printed on transparent material are available, and it's possible to hold the two colours together and check exactly what colour you will achieve.

If you use the **process colours** (cyan, yellow, magenta and black) the colours can be gauged more accurately. These are the tried and tested shades which are used throughout the print industry to produce the full spectrum of colours in four-colour work. Charts showing the colours that can be achieved are much more readily available. Here again, don't forget to overlay tints as well as solids to get as wide a range of colours as possible.

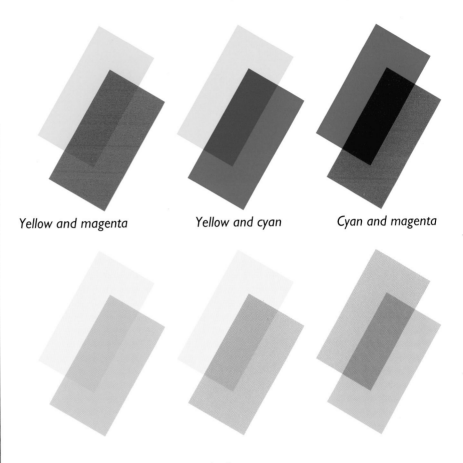

Yellow and magenta   Yellow and cyan   Cyan and magenta

50% tints of the same colours, overlaid

As discussed earlier, two-colour work was traditionally presented as a black and white drawing with an **overlay** showing the areas where the second colour, and its tints, were to be. The expense of hand-cutting the tinted and coloured areas by a **repro house** meant that the budget usually dictated a fairly simple use of the second colour. Now that the illustrator can issue positive film separations direct to the client, the options are limitless. The computer has the capacity to produce graduated tints, subtle blends and radial tints, which would be time-consuming if tackled conventionally. This all adds to the illustrator's armoury of techniques. A richness of image can now be achieved which would have been totally impossible a decade ago.

Three-colour printing

This isn't used very frequently – when one has gone to the expense of using three colours, why not run to four? However, it does crop up occasionally. Many of the points we've discussed in two-colour work apply equally to three-colour printing, i.e. clean, bright colours can be printed on top of one another to create a further one; don't forget to use tints of all the colours; if one of the colours is black, or a fairly dark tone, it will give stronger definition.

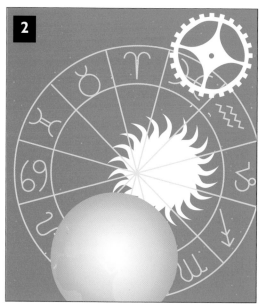

1 shows the yellow plate, 2 cyan, 3 black, and 4 the finished result

The strawberry tarts image had to be produced quickly. Three colours were to be used, so yellow, magenta and black were chosen from the process range. The work was presented to the printer as positive film separations from the computer, and it was printed, trimmed and distributed within 48 hours.

Four-colour printing

As mentioned earlier, the whole spectrum of colours can be created from just four colours – cyan (blue/green), magenta (pinkish red), yellow and black. Again, inspection with a magnifying glass will reveal that the image is a fine pattern of dots, in varying amounts of each of the colours.

Cyan, at 105°

Magenta, at 75°

Yellow, at 90°

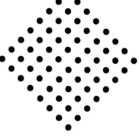

Black, at 45°

The dots are arranged at very precise angles to each other. The dominant colours – cyan, magenta and black – make up a smooth rosette pattern. The tiniest variation in the angles of these can give unexpected results: an interference pattern is created, and the resulting printed image can have a woven or wavy appearance. This is called **moiré** or **screen clash**. The yellow separation – being a less dominant colour – is less crucial. If you want to check the possibility of screen clash in any film separations you may produce, put the magenta, black and cyan films together and hold them up to a light source; you should see a smooth pattern of dots. Don't include the yellow separation in this experiment, as it always produces an interference pattern which isn't perceptible in the printed result because of the less dominant nature of the colour.

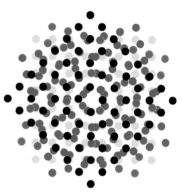

Colour illustration produced on the computer and played out as separations.

*From **The Driving Manual**, (HMSO/DSA).*

Colour illustrations were traditionally produced as a full colour image in whatever medium was chosen – coloured pencils, watercolours, oils, acrylic and so on – before being scanned or photographed at a repro house to be split into the four colour film separations. The computer has opened up a much more economical route, both financially and in labour terms. Full-colour illustrations can be created on screen, checked as colour laser proofs, and run out directly as the four film separations.

Again, the illustrator has had to take on the responsibility previously shouldered by the repro house, but the advantages are great and the drawbacks few. Many clients can now afford full colour illustration where it was previously out of the question, so there is the gain of an increased volume of work. The computer is proving itself to be a very reliable tool in all respects, and the production of good, reliable colour separations (with no screen clash) can be taken for granted.

An illustration given to the client (an author/designer) on disk to be pasted into his work electronically.

From **The Driving Manual,** *(HMSO/DSA).*

This diagram was given to the client in the form of positive film separations, run out directly from the computer.

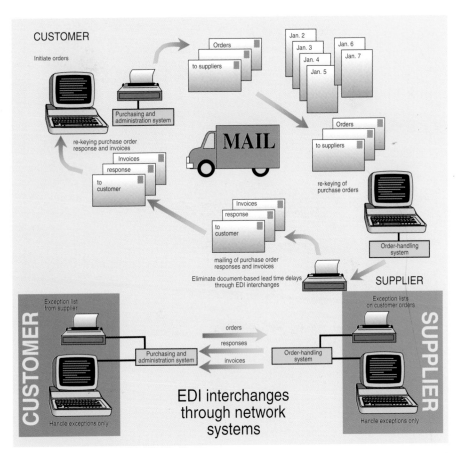

EDI interchanges through network systems

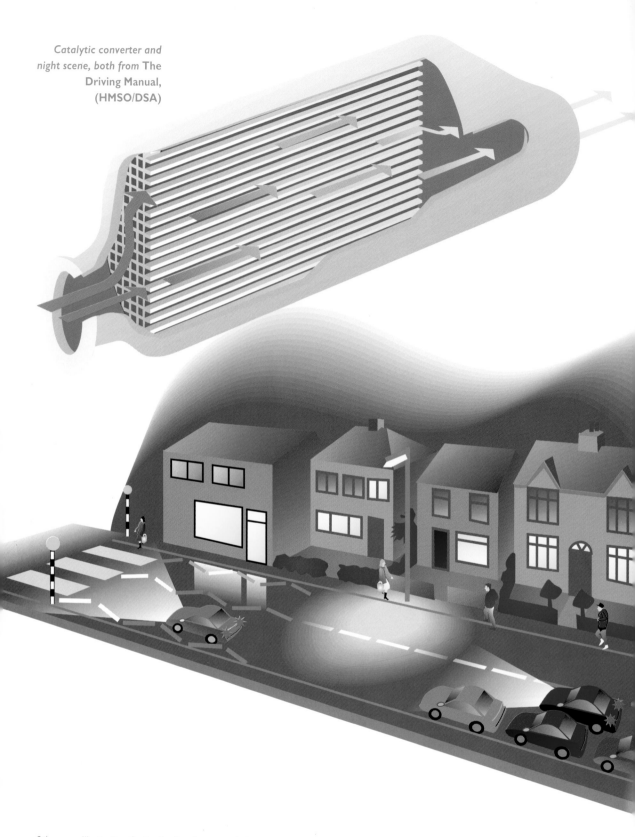

Catalytic converter and night scene, both from **The Driving Manual**, (HMSO/DSA)

More than four-colour printing

This is very high quality printing, where no expense is spared. Perhaps a client has a special Pantone colour that is used throughout the company stationery, and wants, for example, an illustration on the front of the annual report. For a very prestigious publication like this, the client may feel that the representation of the company colour made from the four process colours is not accurate enough, and will specify that the Pantone colour is printed in addition to the four process colours.

Perhaps gold or silver ink is required, which will need to be printed in a separate pass to the process colours. Another very attractive technique is to **spot varnish** areas of the illustration. Varnish is printed onto areas of the image in a separate pass through the press. This gives added depth and richness where applied – almost a wet look.

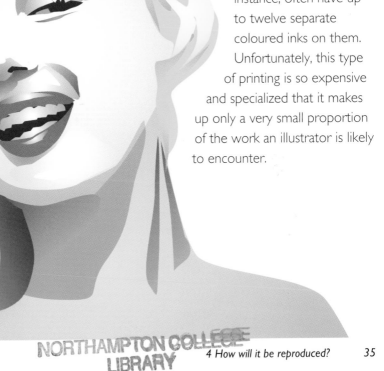

These extra passes through the press – inks over and above the four process colours – are often called **specials**, and the amount of specials one can use is limited only by the artist's imagination and the client's budget. Postage stamps, for instance, often have up to twelve separate coloured inks on them. Unfortunately, this type of printing is so expensive and specialized that it makes up only a very small proportion of the work an illustrator is likely to encounter.

5 How much time has been allowed?

Time is a very important aspect of illustration, in fact, from your client's point of view, probably the most important. From the artist's point of view, there is always less time than you would like! In the commercial world, it is the illustrator's function to produce the best results in the shortest possible time. There are a number of factors which can help this process.

Good reference

Good, clear reference is absolutely essential. Sometimes you will be illustrating a product of some sort, and the client will provide you with the item to take back to your studio and draw from life. Perhaps it's a little larger, and you will have to draw it on site. Or perhaps you will be provided with photographs. For a technical illustration, photographs are probably the least useful of these options; it's surprising how many difficult-to-discern details lurk in the shadows on a photograph. In this case it's probably best to have a glance at the real item if at all possible, and take notes about some of the more important details. You can then work with the photos back at your studio, but use your notes to fill in the gaps.

A public library is the most comprehensive source of general reference, where you should be able to find a visual representation of just about anything. Unfortunately, the public library has two major drawbacks: it involves a journey away from your studio (with all the associated time-consuming problems of getting there, parking, and so on) and it has limited opening hours. These two factors render the library virtually useless for a busy, professional illustrator.

Much more convenient is the option of building up your own reference library at home. It's safe to assume that you enjoy illustrated books (or you wouldn't be reading this one!), so I'm sure a quick glance along your bookshelves will show you have at least the nucleus of your own reference library. Add to this a good encyclopedia, if you don't already have one, and you will have a comprehensive range of reference material. An encyclopedia is expensive, but if you intend to be a life-long, full-time illustrator it will pay for itself time and time again. It doesn't have to be brand-new to be of enormous value – if money is limited, it's worth hunting around for a second-hand one. It's now possible to buy encyclopedia computer programs, and these are also comparatively cheap. The most important benefit of having your own reference library is that it is always available; it is surprising how often, while working at night with a morning deadline fast approaching, reference is suddenly needed for – say – the Golden Temple of Amritsar, or the Empire

State Building. An encyclopedia can save you from missing deadlines on countless occasions.

Children's reference books are also a fine source of visual information. They are often highly pictorial with many clear illustrations and diagrams. Magazines and newspapers are also sometimes useful, but in a more limited fashion. They are so general in content that you often have to scan through many pages before you find anything relevant.

The camera

One trap to be avoided is to become bogged down looking through books and magazines trying to find someone doing exactly the right thing in exactly the right position. This can be a very frustrating experience; sometimes you find that you have spent two hours hunting for reference for an illustration for which you have only allowed three hours in total. With experience, it is possible to decide at the outset where accurate images will be too hard to find in random searches through magazines and so on. Illustrations of how to use specialized equipment or how to perform a specific task fall into this category. If you are commissioned to do a series of pictures showing how to bake a cake, for example, reach for the camera straight away! Enlist a friend or relative as a model, and shoot all the pictures you require. Very fast film-processing laboratories are becoming more and more

Sequence of illustrations showing steps in making beer at home. A quick photographic session was set up first to produce accurate reference for the specialized actions.

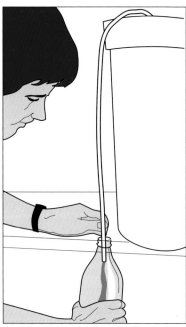

commonplace, and it is possible to be back in your studio with a complete set of totally accurate reference in under two hours. You could easily spend this amount of time hunting through magazines. The finished result is also much better.

'Image grabbers'

The first problem that becomes apparent when using a computer is how to get the basic framework of an image on to the screen. Conventionally, you would do rough sketches and then trace over them on a semi-transparent drafting film, or on to paper by illuminating them from behind with a **light box**. A **scanner** attached to your computer can also help a great deal. Images can be scanned straight onto the screen and traced, as one would with tracing paper over a photograph. **Still video cameras** are now coming onto the market; with these you can take a series of pictures which you can then display on your TV or computer screen. This means you can set up your own reference shots as previously described with a conventional camera, but you can start working with them on the computer straight away. These are expensive at the moment, but – as with all technology – they will rapidly improve in quality and decrease in price. A still video camera is likely to become a very viable and useful purchase for the illustrator in the very near future.

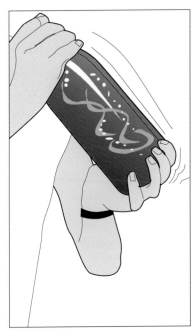

To those of us who remember being taunted at school with 'Oh, but you only traced it', this is all probably beginning to sound very much like cheating! It shouldn't be regarded in this way at all; these are only methods for rapidly getting the **bare bones** of an illustration into the computer. Choice of image, colour, style, line thickness – in fact the full creative input of the illustrator – are still the most important aspects. As with all technology, these methods should be regarded as a way of freeing you from drudgery. They liberate the artist from the mechanics of creating a picture – struggling to get the proportions of the human figure correct, for example – and allow you to concentrate on the more creative aspects in your own particular way. As a commercial illustrator, your task is to convey your client's message as originally and powerfully as possible; the final result should be a distillation of your own ideas and experience, closely allied to your client's ideas. The fact that you copy and trace various elements doesn't detract from this. It's necessary to use everything in your power to achieve the best possible finished result.

It's important here to emphasise the distinction between the tracing techniques described – time-saving methods to get an accurate framework onto the computer screen – and plagiarism. Plagiarism is the wholesale copying of ideas, and should be avoided at all costs. It is deeply unsatisfying to the artist who commits it, and can lead to bitter copyright battles.

The mirror

Don't forget one important source of reference for the human figure that is always available to you – yourself. With the aid of a mirror you can use yourself as a model quite successfully. If you are having difficulty with a certain stance or pose, even without a mirror it's often helpful to get into that pose yourself. It's very useful to get the 'feel' of it – to decide where your weight is being supported, what angle your hips and shoulders are at, and so on.

Substitutes

Use household objects as a substitute for items that are not available to you. Build up a street scene with cardboard boxes, and give it some directional lighting with an adjustable lamp; oranges can be models for planets in an illustration of the solar system. These tricks will help you to render the light and shade more accurately, and give an illustration a more life like feel.

The computer

The computer itself is the biggest time-saving device. Don't forget to save everything you do. With **floppy disks, removable drives, optical storage** and so on, this need take up very little space in your studio. (The various hardware storage options are evolving constantly, and are thus outside the scope of this book; a computer dealer, or up-to-date computer magazine will give you a good idea of what is currently available). Computer programs are available to compress the information still further, so several years' work need only take up a foot or so of shelf space. There is no need to throw anything away.

All the images you generate become your **clip art library**. You can take a previously-generated image, colour it, change the line weight, distort and duplicate it, and create a completely new illustration.

Let's try it with the butterfly image used earlier in this book.

1. Distort one wing, to give it a little movement.

2. Duplicate it.

3. Flip the butterfly over 90° (mirror-image).

4. Reduce it.

5. Duplicate and reduce several more times.

6. Draw in the butterflies' food plant.

Create a few more flower heads, by duplicating your first flower, changing its size and mirror-imaging it (as you did with the butterflies). Drop in a simple background of a graduated tint of blue, and you have a whole new illustration, completed in under an hour.

The production team

Armed with these time-saving techniques, you must also consider yourself as part of a team. Your illustration will not stand in isolation – it will be reproduced in a publication along with other material. Let's take a quick look at the processes involved in colour publication production.

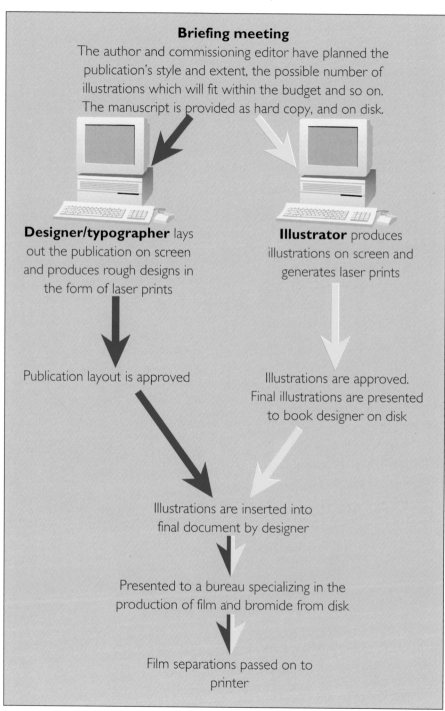

Briefing meeting
The author and commissioning editor have planned the publication's style and extent, the possible number of illustrations which will fit within the budget and so on. The manuscript is provided as hard copy, and on disk.

Designer/typographer lays out the publication on screen and produces rough designs in the form of laser prints

Illustrator produces illustrations on screen and generates laser prints

Publication layout is approved

Illustrations are approved. Final illustrations are presented to book designer on disk

Illustrations are inserted into final document by designer

Presented to a bureau specializing in the production of film and bromide from disk

Film separations passed on to printer

As you can see, everything is interdependent. If you let your deadlines slip, you could easily find yourself in the embarassing position of holding up the entire publication.

The computer has given us the advantage of being able to make corrections quickly and easily, right up to the very last stage of production. In the past, once an illustration was in its final form on paper or board, it was difficult – in some cases impossible – to make alterations. New areas could be spliced in or pasted over, but it was generally avoided unless absolutely necessary. With the computer, laser prints are presented to the client, and these are progressively refined until they meet the client's requirements; elements can be moved, enlarged, deleted and so on. Unfortunately this advantage is double-edged. There is no longer a clear cut-off point where the illustration is regarded as finished. You can find yourself making quite major changes until the eve of publication. Your client may often not fully understand that although alterations can be made relatively quickly, they still take time. Many computer-illustrators and typesetters must have quaked at the words 'it's only a matter of pressing a few buttons, isn't it?'. However, do remember that it is the client's prerogative to make changes until the work has total approval. You should mentally allow yourself more time for the latter stages of a job than you would at first suppose; a good rule of thumb is to estimate how long you imagine it will take and then double it! Don't be afraid to keep the client in the picture by stating, firmly but politely, when you consider that the illustration is reaching completion, and at what point further changes will become difficult and expensive.

Looking back to our diagram you will see that when the work is finally approved it is handed to the book designer on disk. It's worth mentioning at this point that it is in your own best interest not to hand over your *original* on disk. By this I mean the document you create in your drawing or painting program. This should be converted to a *read-only* format, such as **EPS, TIFF** or **PICT**. A book designer may not have the illustration program you have used, and will need the file in this universal form to incorporate it into the text.

Secondly, if you hand over an original work an unscrupulous person may be able to take it apart and use it to create new illustrations (as we did with the butterfly on pp 31-33). This is a new pitfall of illustration as a profession which has been created by the computer. In the past an illustration could be used in more than one publication by the client, but it had to be used in its entirety; the client had purchased the illustration as a finite image. With computer technology it's possible to use selected parts, duplicate them, transform them and so on. The clip art library that you generate during the course of your work is **your** property and **your** asset. If a client wants you to provide the original on disk, so that it can be altered by someone else at a future date, you should negotiate a much higher fee. In this instance you are not giving away a finite illustration with a limited use, but a template from which many further illustrations could possibly be created. You must be fully aware of the difference in value between original and read-only documents. This is such new territory that it's easy for a client and an illustrator, with no malicious intent whatsoever, to fall foul of each other. A client may offer to help by doing the final corrections to the originals in house, on the client's own computer, to take the pressure off you. You may be so overworked that you hand over the originals with a sigh of relief. After some time, your client may give your work on disk to another illustrator, as examples. The illustrator, quite unaware of the original contract you had with the client, may use elements you originated in some new illustrations. Imagine how galling it would be to open a publication and find images you had struggled to create juxtaposed differently in a new illustration! It's best to protect yourself and your client against this possibility by making it a hard-and-fast rule always to issue your work on disk in a read-only format.

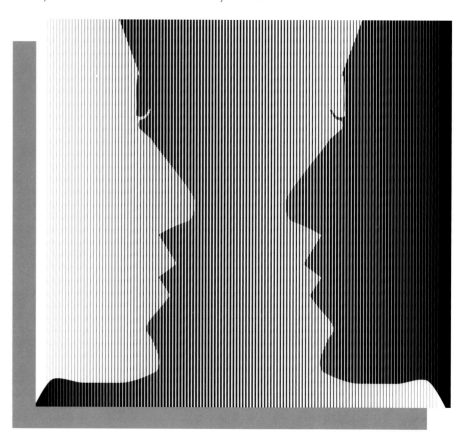

Illustration from a book cover: **The Listening Manager.**

The client's budget

You must make sure that you understand exactly what the client wants, in terms of price and complexity. It's no good producing a very elaborate, costly illustration when the budget only allows for something quite simple. A client would be extremely annoyed if he or she commissioned you to do a job that was estimated to take only an hour or two of your time, and was then presented with a beautiful, intricate illustration and an invoice for a week's work! On the other hand you will get no thanks for producing a quick, inexpensive illustration when you have been commissioned to produce something very elaborate for a prestigious publication. This must be one of the most difficult areas for the novice illustrator, and one that only becomes easier with experience. You must obtain a very accurate idea of what a client wants, and how much money there is to pay for it. It's best to make sure at the briefing meeting exactly what everyone expects from the contract. Don't forget that it's much better to ask embarrassing questions than to make embarrassing mistakes!

6 What are your own particular skills?

Now we come to the last and most important part of the process – YOU.

No illustrator is good at every subject and style. It's worth pausing for a while to analyse your own strengths and weaknesses. Why not jot down a quick list, in two columns? This is the beginning of mine:

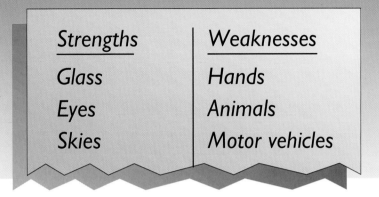

Strengths	*Weaknesses*
Glass	*Hands*
Eyes	*Animals*
Skies	*Motor vehicles*

Having recognized your weaknesses, don't just use it as an excuse for turning down every project that contains them from now on! With good reference you should be able to make a professional job of anything you may encounter.

Some piano-playing hands for a maths textbook –only one hand was drawn, and the others were created by duplicating the first, flipping it over and changing the colour.

The computer is a great asset in this. I find that I enjoy drawing profiles which are facing left, but have tremendous difficulty with those facing right. (On discussion, this seems to be shared with many artists – perhaps it's a phenomenon linked to left- or right-handedness.) Now, I comfortably draw everyone facing left, and flip the image where necessary. A difficult item, like a hand, need only be drawn once and can then be duplicated and transformed for further use.

Try to approach the commission with a very positive mental attitude. Perhaps you have to draw a horse, which might happen to be your worst subject! Find a good reference and trace the image, then go one step further and try to add something which you are very good at. You may be particularly skilled at creating the look of leather, for instance; add a beautifully-observed saddle or harness.

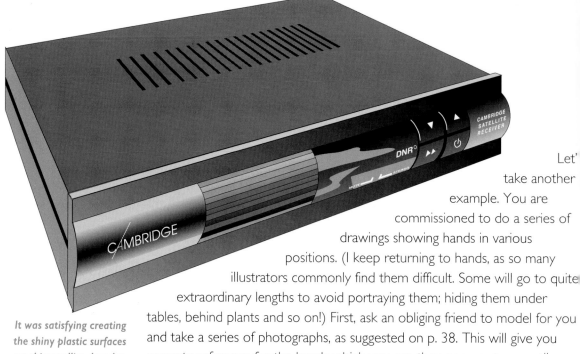

It was satisfying creating the shiny plastic surfaces on this satellite decoder.

Let' take another example. You are commissioned to do a series of drawings showing hands in various positions. (I keep returning to hands, as so many illustrators commonly find them difficult. Some will go to quite extraordinary lengths to avoid portraying them; hiding them under tables, behind plants and so on!) First, ask an obliging friend to model for you and take a series of photographs, as suggested on p. 38. This will give you accurate reference for the hands which you can then copy or trace until you have a satisfactory image. Then go one step further and add your own particular dash of excellence. Perhaps you are very good at rendering glass and metal surfaces; why not add a finely-drawn watch, complete with rich reflections? Illustrations can be lifted from the ordinary to the inspired by just one or two really well-observed details like this.

Bring your own special talents into every illustration you create. Of course, it's not advisable to stray too far from the original brief. Your client will not be thrilled if presented with a picture of a steam locomotive, just because you happen to be particularly good at rendering steam and vapour, when the commission was for a modern railway scene! It's not necessary to go to these lengths – everything you are commissioned to do can be made to include images that you particularly enjoy creating. Enjoyment is the key word. If you enjoyed working on a particular aspect of an illustration, it will often be conveyed to the observer. Notice how often you show an illustration to a client or friend and they comment on the very aspect you most enjoyed creating.

To sum up, accentuate your strengths, and get good reference for areas in which you are weak.

No longer a blank sheet

Having answered the six key questions, I hope you now find that you have built up a fairly solid framework within which to work – that blank sheet of paper should no longer look quite so daunting!

You can now clear your mind of things which are inappropriate for the current project.

To recap, your illustration needs to convey what your client wants to say; keep this central in your mind, along with your idea of the potential 'customer' who will be looking at it. Your illustration needs to be ready on time, and within budget. It needs to reproduce well, taking into consideration the advantages and disadvantages of the techniques by which it will be printed, and the surface it will be printed on. When you are fully satisfied that these demands will be met, don't forget to add a good dash of your own particular strengths and enjoyment!

Now let's work through some real-life case studies, applying these principles.

*The illustration on the right is from **The Motorcycle Manual**, to be printed in full colour on good quality paper. The requirements were quite different for the house illustration below, which was for a newspaper advertisement.*

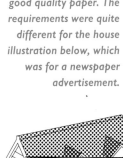

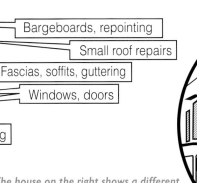

Bargeboards, repointing

Small roof repairs

Fascias, soffits, guttering

Windows, doors

Cladding

The house on the right shows a different style; this was for a letterhead and was therefore given a much more elegant and delicate treatment.

INTRA COUNTRY TRADE IN CHOCOLATE

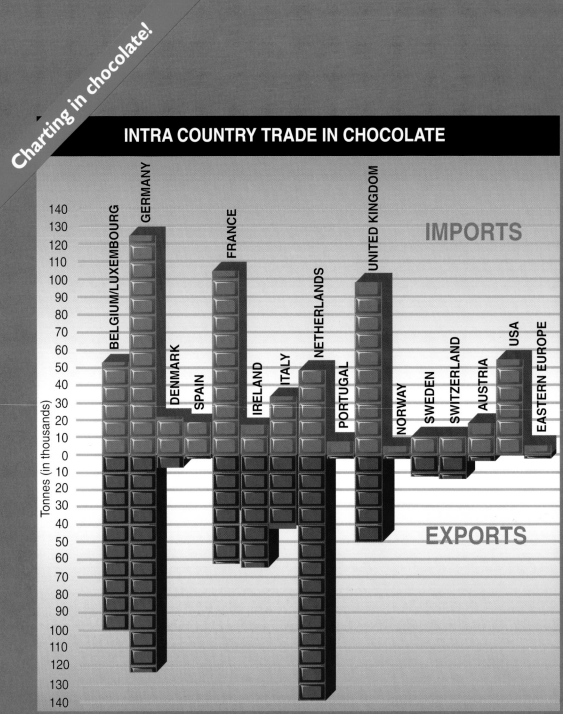

IMPORTS

EXPORTS

Tonnes (in thousands)

BELGIUM/LUXEMBOURG
GERMANY
DENMARK
SPAIN
FRANCE
IRELAND
ITALY
NETHERLANDS
PORTUGAL
UNITED KINGDOM
NORWAY
SWEDEN
SWITZERLAND
AUSTRIA
USA
EASTERN EUROPE

140 130 120 110 100 90 80 70 60 50 40 30 20 10 0 10 20 30 40 50 60 70 80 90 100 110 120 130 140

INTRA COUNTRY TRADE IN CHOCOLATE figures in tonnes (in thousands)	Imports	Exports
Belgium/Luxembourg	53	100
Germany	125	123
Denmark	22	8
Spain	19	2
France	105	63
Ireland	17	65
Italy	33	42
Netherlands	48	140
Portugal	7	2
United Kingdom	98	51
Norway	5	2
Sweden	10	12
Switzerland	10	15
Austria	18	5
USA	54	1
Eastern Europe	5	2

The information for this job came through the post as a batch of typewritten statistics to be made up into a number of charts. The client and I had built up a good rapport in several previous projects, and it wasn't necessary to meet in person or discuss the material further on the phone. I knew from experience that a quick turn-around and a lively style were required. Although the chart had to be accurate, its main function wasn't pure instruction so some embellishment was called for.

After some consideration, I was able to apply the six questions to the brief and come up with the following answers:

1. Purpose?
To enliven some dense text in a magazine-type publication.

2. Who is it for?
Managing directors, marketing managers, financial directors of large companies who are likely to be busy, so it's important that the chart is eye-catching.

3. For how long will it be seen?
A quarterly publication, so quite ephemeral – a fashionable approach would be acceptable.

4. How will it be reproduced?
Full colour, to be presented as postive film separations.

5. Budget/Time?
The text was ready and waiting to be laid out around the diagrams in this publication, so maximum speed was essential.

6. Your particular skills
I enjoy creating the variety of textures occurring in food, from silky, semi-matt surfaces to glossy, transparent jellies and sauces.

Illustration

A short brain-storming session produced the idea of depicting the tonnes as squares of chocolate – milk chocolate showing imports, and plain chocolate depicting exports. The challenge of rendering the luscious gloss of chocolate was very stimulating, and full use could be made of the smooth graduations at which the computer excels. There was also the added advantage of only needing to draw one square of chocolate, which could then be duplicated as many times as necessary.

The first step was to construct the basic skeleton of the chart. A special chart program was useful at this point; the figures were simply typed in, and then could be translated by the computer into pie, graph, column or bar chart. This saved a lot of time and improved accuracy by eliminating the chore of constructing the outline of the chart. On many occasions it's possible to take the original chart and transform it, by adding colour, drop shadows and so on, but in this instance it was just being used as a guide.

Here we have the 'imports' typed in and displayed as a column chart in the chart program:

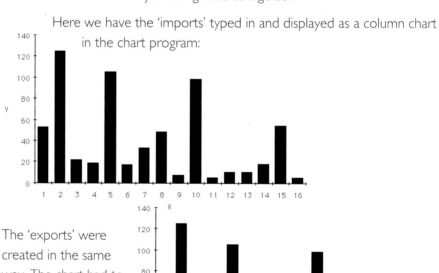

The 'exports' were created in the same way. The chart had to be flipped to a mirror image, and moved into position below the original:

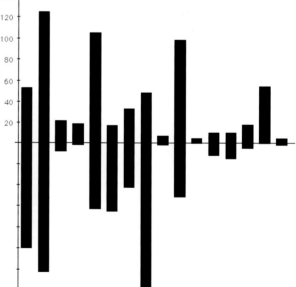

As the images so far created were to be used only as a guide, it was necessary to move them to a 'backgound' layer (a layer which either doesn't print at all, or which can be isolated and removed at a later stage – see *Technical tip*).

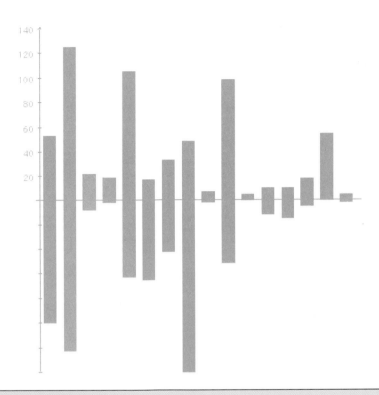

Technical tip

It greatly increases ease of working if you have a computer illustration program which allows you to construct 'layers' within an illustration. (This concept is easy to grasp if you imagine that you are creating different elements of your picture on a sequence of transparent sheets which can be pulled out and worked on individually, and then reassembled at the end to form the complete illustration.) This allows you to construct a rough grid or outline on a non-printing background layer, which you can then use to trace over on a higher layer.

It's good practice to put background and foreground details on different layers, too; if you are then asked to correct a background detail it will be easy to isolate that layer and work on it separately. It's often difficult – and sometimes impossible – to sift your way through a mass of foreground details if you have constructed everything on the same layer.

Any text should ideally go on a separate, topmost layer, as this is often the element which needs the most correction.

The figure shows a simple construction of layers; it's often possible to have as many as you wish. As your work becomes more and more complex you will find it useful to set a little time aside to plan how many layers you are going to create, and what you are going to put on each.

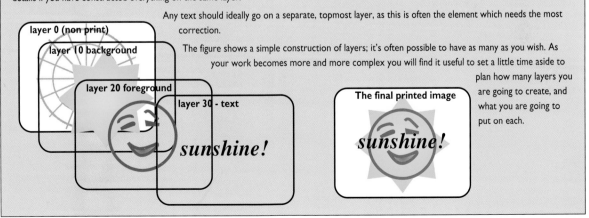

Once the grid lines were created, the next job was to create a palette of colours for the dark and milk chocolate squares. The basic brown was mixed in each case, then copied and the colour deepened to produce a shade for dark areas. A tint of the brown was made for the highlights, where white would also be used.

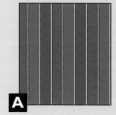
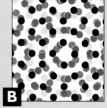

The detail on a single square was built up in the following sequence:

This supplied the basic building block for the chart. It was duplicated and the colours changed to produce a dark chocolate square.

The chart could then be built up using the background as a guide.

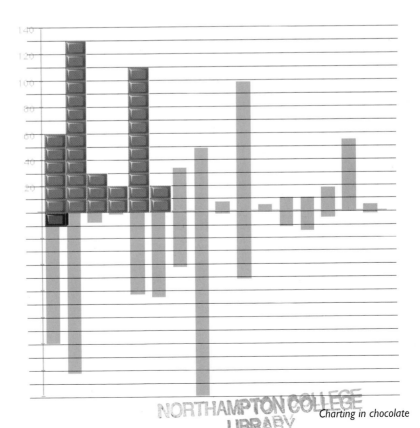

When complete, the dark brown sides of the chocolate columns were added, to give a chunky three-dimensional effect. The grid lines were thickened and changed to grey, to give a more subtle, yet still visible, effect.

The background was then added, made up of two slabs of blue tint, graduating to white at the middle. This was chosen for two reasons. Firstly, the graduation gave a more lively background. Secondly, it gave the viewer a visual clue – the deeper the background, the higher the tonnage – to help convey the sense of the chart.

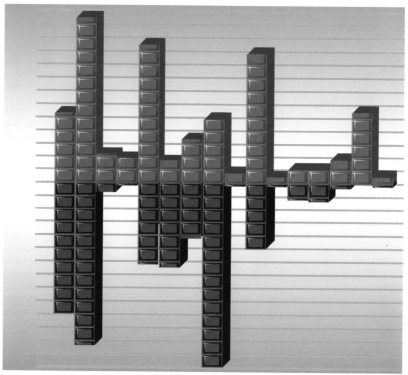

Finally, the text was added (on the topmost layer, as suggested in the *Technical tip*, p. 53), and the chart was complete.

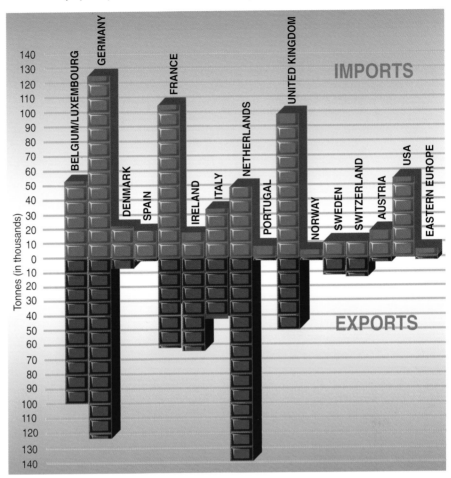

This wasn't quite the end of the story, however. The chart was then presented to the client in the form of a laser print. Fortunately, they liked the basic concept, so there were no major changes, but there were a couple of small typographical errors which were indicated on a copy and faxed back. The final corrections were implemented and approved, also by fax.

At this point, **registration marks** were added around the figure, and the completed file copied onto a floppy disk and presented to a **bureau**. The four positive film separations were produced overnight, and presented to the client the following morning to be stripped in to the rest of the page, prior to plate-making.

A woodcut approach

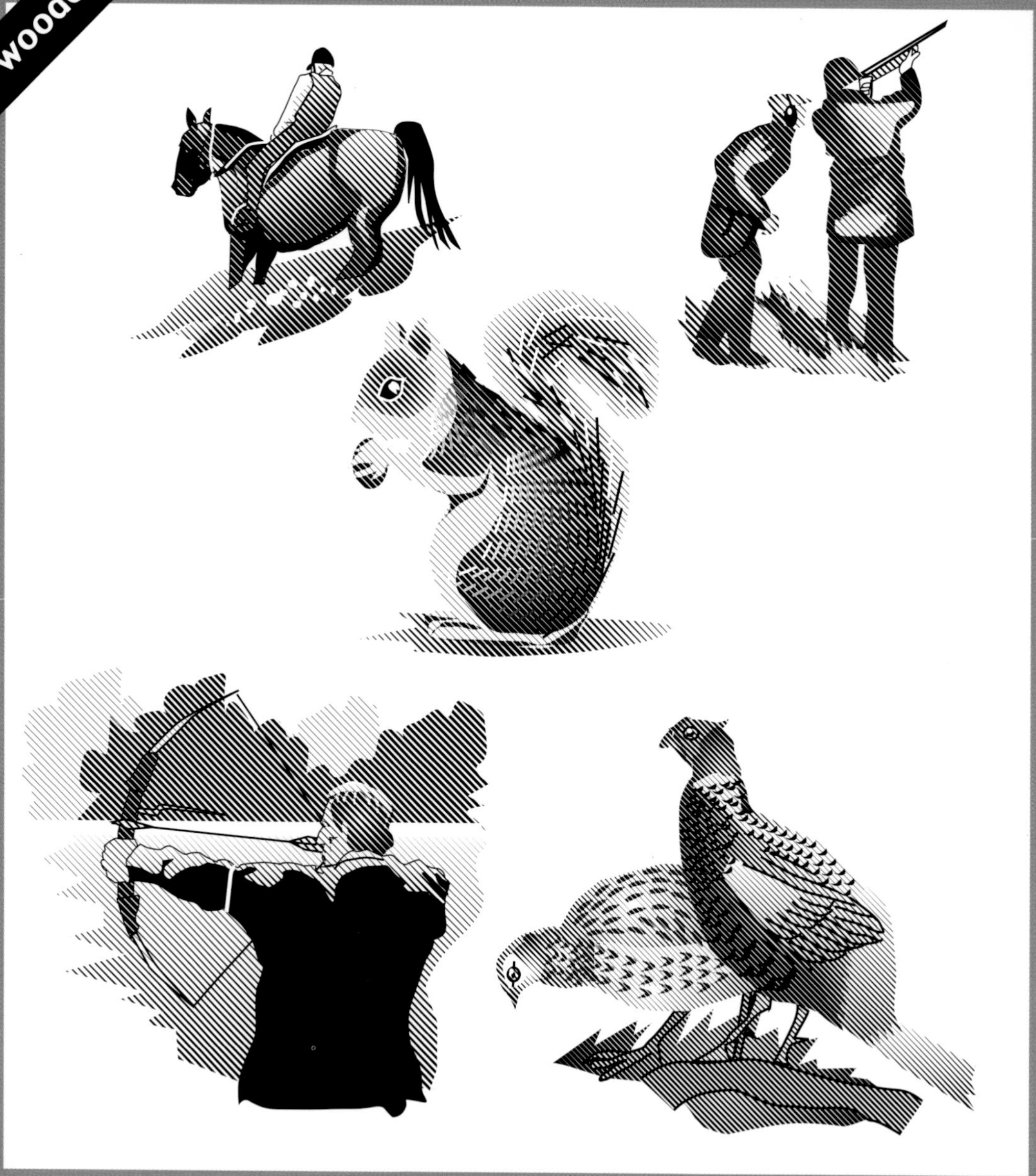

This project was discussed at a person-to-person meeting. I wasn't dealing directly with the customer – the proprietor of a distinguished country hotel – but with a printer who had secured both the design and print of the job.

There was a rough mock-up produced by the client and two visuals by other illustrators which had been rejected. This situation, which occurs quite often, can have both positive and negative aspects. On the positive side, it gives you a clear idea of what the client doesn't like, which, by a process of elimination, can clarify your view of the task. On the other hand, it could indicate that the client is excessively demanding and will reject everything presented to him! One of the rejected visuals showed a clean, modern design, using photographs of the hotel. The second had an elegant art-deco design. Both were attractive and well-executed, but they obviously didn't convey the image of the hotel that the proprietor wanted. What could that be? Perhaps answers to our six key questions could help:

1. Purpose?
For a leaflet advertising a large, exclusive country hotel.

2. Who is it for?
The hotel customer would probably be the traditional type. Possibly someone living a busy life in the city, wanting to get away for a few days of relaxation in a peaceful country environment.

6. Your particular skills
The subject matter had many areas of difficulty – particularly horses and people in sporting poses. On the other hand, it was going to be easy to find clear reference.

3. For how long will it be seen?
Quite ephemeral – a lifespan of not more than a year or so.

5. Budget/Time?
This was quite generous – about two hours per illustration.

4. How will it be reproduced?
In two colours on textured and/or coloured paper. A bold approach would be best, with no fine lines or tints.

We took a first glance at radial and graduated tints back on p 23, but they are such a useful part of computer illustration that it's worth examining them further.

Remember that a radial tint can look effective within a shaped outline …

…or repeated in irregular shapes for waves, or distant mountains.

The highlight, even on a circle, needn't always be in the middle…

…and graduated tints make fine shadows.

Graduating an image out to white at the edge can be an interesting way of indicating the continuation of an item:

The hotel had the words 'country house' in its name, and the logo on its stationery showed a hotel nestling in extensive grounds. The rough mock-up indicated that several country pursuits were available at or nearby the hotel: pony-trekking, archery, shooting and nature rambling. These clues led me to believe that the hotel wanted to present itself as an elegant and traditional country retreat. This was possibly where the two other designs had failed – the first was too modern, and the second, art-deco version was perhaps more suited to a sophisticated, urban establishment.

I found myself thinking of the woodcuts of Thomas Bewick (1753-1828); they have a rich, historic countryside feel to them, and are strong with densely textured areas and solid, velvety blacks. Something with a similar feel would look good on the coloured and textured paper favoured by the client.

Five images were required in all – an illustration for each of the four country pursuits and a further one as a stylish finishing point at the end of the text. The client had indicated a squirrel for this, and I felt this would be a good starting point. I soon found reference in a children's book (from my home library) and did a simple trace of the main features. I scanned this into the computer, putting it onto a non-print background layer, and began work using the scan as a guide.

The outline was created.

Then the main dark areas.

A radial tint worked well here, indicating the roundness of the squirrel's body.

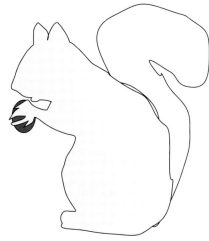

The eye is always important.
Time spent creating a good
shine and accurate positioning
of a highlight can help a great
deal in giving life to a creature.

The large, delicate fluffy tail is one of the squirrel's main features, and it was
important to get the right effect. A dark core was created, and blended out to
the paler grey outline. This gave the right amount of softness, but the result
was perhaps a little too bland.

Straight strokes were dashed in, in black and white. These contrasted with the softness and gave an indication of the brindle quality of a squirrel's tail.

Now the body looked a little too smooth. Perhaps it could benefit from the same treatment?

A white dotted line was added towards the front of the squirrel, and a black dotted line drawn in to accentuate the spine. They were then blended together, in twelve steps, by the computer. This gave the impression of fur and also accentuated the round shape of the squirrel's body.

Technical tips

The blend technique is another computer speciality, worth exploiting to the full. It can produce intriguing, dramatic effects; experiment with it until you are fully satisfied with the results.

Lines of different shapes and the same colour can be blended...

The number of steps can be chosen by the illustrator – either very few...

Different shapes can be blended...

...and different shapes of different colours:-

...or lines of different colours:

...or many:

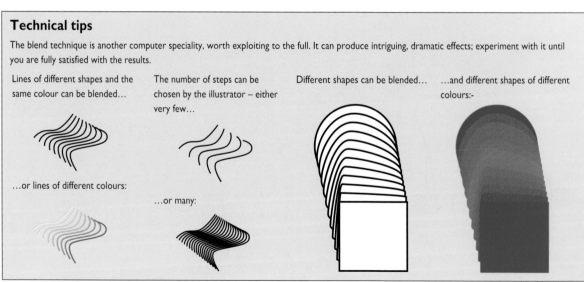

Inspired by the success of this technique, I added a further blend on the neck and shoulders.

The illustration was now complete. However, the tints were still too fine for the intended paper surface. I instructed the computer to reproduce the tints in the form of lines, at a coarse frequency of 35 per inch. On a true woodcut, the lines of tinting would follow the form of the image. This wasn't possible in the program I was using, but the line tint was nonetheless quite successful; the image had a similar chunky, dense quality.

I was pleased with this illustration, and felt it set the tone for the remaining images. These were built up in the same way; good reference was found, traced, scanned and used as a basic framework. The blend technique was used several more times, most successfully on the shoulders of the sportsman with the gun.

Texture was added to the pheasants by indicating the feather patterning; only one dark scallop shape had to be constructed, and this was then duplicated as often as required.

When complete, all the illustrations were given the same coarse line screen.

The client was delighted with the resulting laser print, and the illustrations were ultimately printed in dark charcoal grey and russet on a grey, marbled paper. The leaflet had a rustic, antique feel which conveyed an atmosphere of tradition, good food and roaring log fires!

This was one of a series of illustrations which was the result of a long briefing meeting with the owner of a small, recently established travel company.

I was dealing with the total design and typesetting of the annual brochure. Transparencies of the holiday properties and venues, and several simple line maps, were already available. Most of the content of the brochure was settled, but the client had several properties at each destination which would not be finalized until just before going to press (as is often the case with holiday brochures). We thought it wise to include zones in the brochure where holiday details could be inserted at the last minute. I suggested that a series of illustrations might fit this purpose; they would make a good contrast to the crisp photographs and stark line maps, and yet could be reduced in size, or deleted altogether, to allow room for last-minute deals.

At this point, let's assess the project:

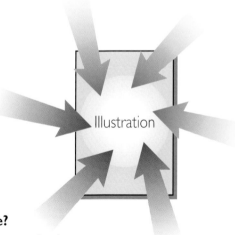

1. Purpose?
To add a contrast to dense pages of colour photos and text. To create flexible areas to allow last minute changes.

2. Who is it for?
Adults, anticipating future treats. Images should be evocative and mood-creating.

6. Your particular skills
Creating the glosses and rich colour of fruit would be stimulating and rewarding.

3. For how long will it be seen?
May be used for several years as the brochure content grows and changes; a very up-to-the-minute style may be inappropriate.

5. Budget/Time?
The client was happy to budget for five or six hours' work on each image initially, as each could have many further uses.

4. How will it be reproduced?
Full-colour, on good quality paper.

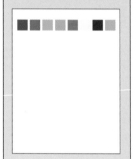

What makes a holiday attractive? Why do we enjoy it? All the senses are involved in the enjoyment of foreign travel, not least of which are taste and smell. Reflecting on my own vacations, I realised that I associated certain foods with different areas. The tomatoes in Corfu, for example, were the best I've ever tasted. Figs and almonds in Mallorca were quite sensational. A quick appraisal of the destinations revealed that a particular food could be associated with each – oranges with Florida, baguettes and brie with France, for instance. I decided to do a still life of local food for each destination, making sure that each image was composed of distinct, individual items. I could then take one or two of the items and reassemble them to make further images if the need arose.

The first step was to set up a still life and produce an accurate pencil drawing.

Then a palette of colours was created, with the help of printed colour charts.

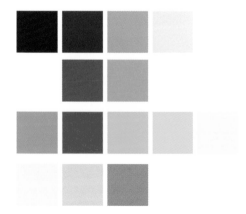

The image had to be transferred to the screen in some way. With no scanner available at the time, a traditional technique was adopted. The image was traced and a grid drawn over it:

An identical grid was created on screen and dropped onto a background layer, then the contents of each square were copied from the paper to the screen. This was the skeleton of the drawing.

The component parts of the illustration needed to be easily isolated to create further illustrations, so some time was given at this point to deciding on which layer each element should be drawn.

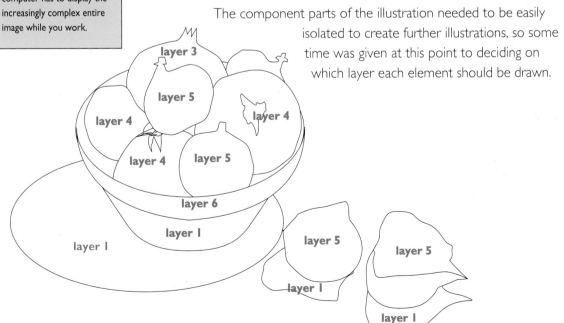

The still life was set up nearby, as a reference for the colours. It was important to give the impression of strong sunlight, to convey a warm, Mediterranean mood, so the composition was closely lit with a lamp. Each fruit was built up individually, starting from the back.

The figs were relatively simple, and patches of radial tints were used to convey the wrinkly, semi-matt surface of the skin.

The pomegranates were more of a problem. The skin is marked with a complex, delicate red streaking, and is highly glossy without being smooth. Many experiments were made before a solution was found.

The red streaks were time consuming to execute, but the task was made easier by duplicating and transforming.

(The figure on the right shows, by highlighting one of the streaks, how the pattern was built up by using the same few basic shapes, which were flipped, tweaked and rotated as necessary.)

The slightly textured nature of the skin meant that the highlight created by the lamp (the substitute Mediterranean sun!) was split into many small slivers. Capturing this effect was going to be the feature that brought the illustration to life.

Laying a white highlight under the red streaking was tried, but this was unsuccessful.

The highlight wasn't fragmented enough, and a close examination of the real fruit showed that the red streaks weren't thrown into relief by the shine in this way.

Perhaps the red streaks themselves could contain the sun's reflection?

A tint graduating from red to white was dropped into some of the streaks. This gave just the required effect. Inspired by this success, I used the technique in reverse on the shaded side of the fruit – graduating the tint from red to dark red. (The ease with which one can experiment is another great advantage of computer illustration. Many different techniques can be tried on a challenging area until the desired effect is created, while satisfactory areas can be left untouched.)

The rest of the fruits were created in the same way.

Another stimulating task was to depict the contents of the fig; the contrast of the pale green seeds with the dull red of the flesh is the factor which evokes this fruit. Another factor is the fibrous look created by the filaments holding the seeds. A pale pink line was created and used freely to draw in these fibres.

Finally, strong shadows were dropped in on the bottom drawing layer, to help strengthen the impression of strong sunlight.

The finished illustration was successful. The initial investment in time proved worthwhile later in the same year when a brochure supplement was produced, and several smaller illustrations were quickly created, linking the imagery with the original brochure.

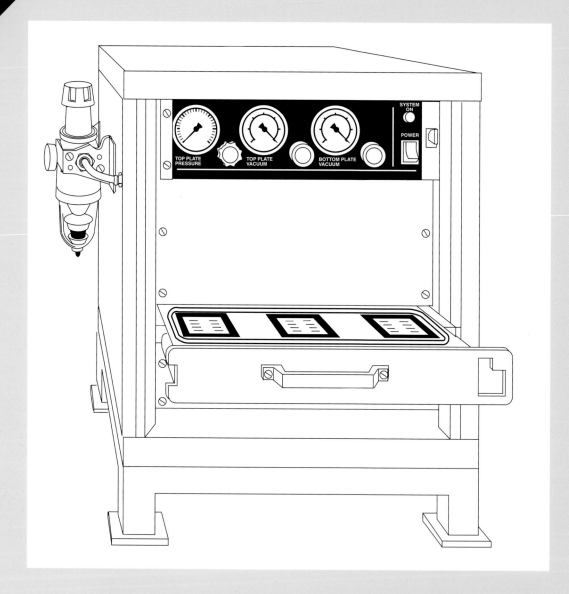

TOP PLATE
PRESSURE

TOP PLATE
VACUUM

BOTTOM PLATE
VACUUM

SYSTEM
ON

POWER

The client for this project was a technical author, who required some clear illustrations for a manual, written to accompany a new piece of equipment. (The device was designed to test the impermeability – or otherwise – of the blister packs which hold medicinal pills). The specialized nature of the machinery meant that the manual had a very short print run, and therefore attractive, clear, well-designed laser prints would be quite adequate as artwork.

As the equipment was so new, there were no existing photographs or literature for use as reference. An appointment was made for me to visit the workshop and draw the machine on site.

Let's apply our six questions to this project:

1. Purpose?
A clear diagram for an instruction manual.

2. Who is it for?
Technicians in the pharmaceutical industry.

6. Your particular skills
The challenge lay in conveying the information clearly.

3. For how long will it be seen?
Possibly several years, so a quirky fashionable style would not be appropriate.

5. Budget/Time?
Three hours.

4. How will it be reproduced?
Black and white. Artwork to be produced as 300 dot per inch laser print.

At the factory I quickly began work. Little attention was paid to the finish of the image – circles were rather wobbly and straight lines were quite curvaceous at times! This didn't matter; back at the computer straight lines could be created in minutes, and circles formed perfectly. The important task was to record the proportions and positions of the various features as accurately as possible.

Recording the relative positions and dimensions was made easier by the traditional technique of using the pencil as a visual ruler. The following figures show how this method works.

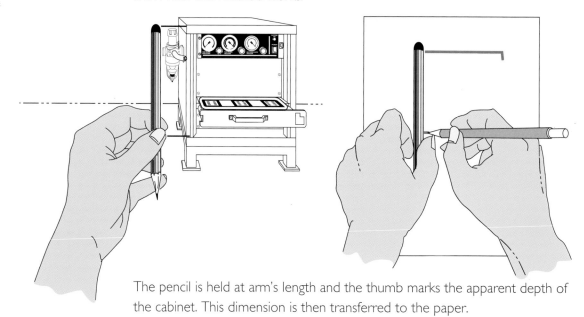

The pencil is held at arm's length and the thumb marks the apparent depth of the cabinet. This dimension is then transferred to the paper.

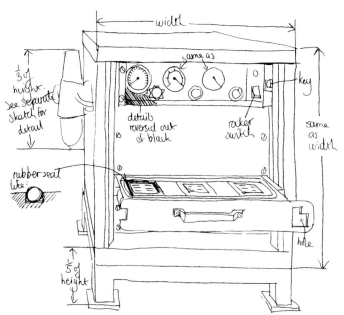

Once the dimensions of the main body of the cabinet had been ascertained, the task became considerably easier. There was now a framework within which to work. The black panel at the top, for example, was roughly a quarter of the depth of the square cabinet. Written notes helped where there was any possible confusion.

The drawer was structurally complicated; the drawer front itself was asymmetrical, with a disproportionate amount of surface protruding on the right hand side. It was necessary to make a mental note of this. It would have been easy to conclude that it was a mistake in the original sketch, and wrongly correct it to a symmetrical shape when working on the final image. In fact, the drawer in the finished illustration looks 'wrong', but is totally accurate, nevertheless.

Back at the office, armed with the sketch and written notes, work commenced on the final artwork. Initially, only the basic elements were drawn on the non-print background layer.

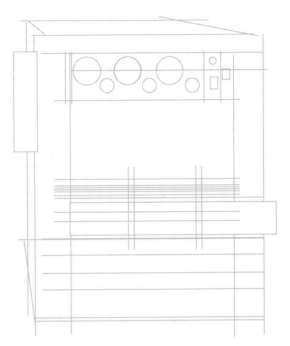

The perspective had to be absolutely correct. The lines delineating the top edge of the cabinet were extended upwards until they met; this was the vanishing point. Further lines could be drawn starting from this point, to give the correct angles for the drawer sides, square feet and so on.

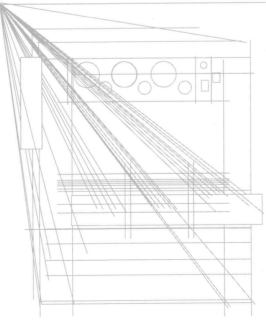

Technical tip

Although many computer-aided design programs are available which portray perspective, this isn't currently a feature of illustration and paint programs. The emphasis in these programs is the achievement of a good printed result. Were a program to contain the necessary information both for the portrayal of perspective and all the details for accurate four-colour reproduction – screen angles, dot size etc. – it would be extremely unwieldy and require such a powerful and expensive machine that it would be out of the range of the pocket of the average illustrator. It is only a matter of time before personal computers develop the necessary speed and power, but at present we have to rely on the traditional techniques.

However, the traditional techniques are much faster and easier with a computer, as shown here...

1. Working in a background, or non-print, layer draw in the horizon. This can extend well off the edges of the document – view it at 25% or 12.5% of its size.

2. Decide the position of your vanishing point and hang a straight line from it.

3. Duplicate the line, select the end (taking care to not pick up the whole line) and pull it round, leaving the other end firmly attached to the vanishing point.

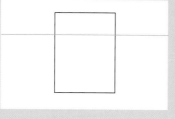

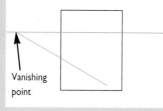

Vanishing point

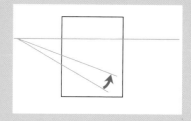

4. Repeat as often as required.

5. Use the grid as a guide for your illustration.

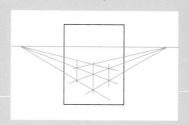

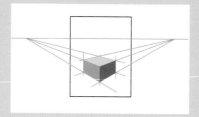

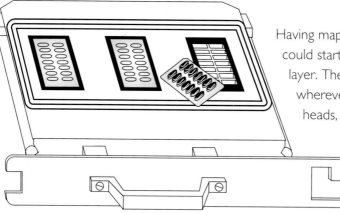

Having mapped out the basic structure, work could start in earnest on a higher, printing layer. The technique of duplication was used wherever possible – on the dials and screw heads, for example – to save time.

A further illustration was required of the drawer on its own, and this was produced in the same style.

Few tints were used in this drawing for two reasons. Firstly, it needed to be as simple and accurate as possible. Its primary function was to convey the necessary details as quickly as possible. The purpose of this image was to instruct, not entertain, so no further embellishment was required. Secondly, the method of reproduction had to be taken into consideration. The artwork was going to be in the form of 300 dots per inch laser prints. Large areas of tint in this medium can be patchy and banded in appearance, so they should be kept to a minimum. Small areas of tint work best. Very fine lines were rejected, too. Finer lines reproduce on the laser print, but the resolution dictates that they are not thinner than approximately 0.2mm. For example, two parallel lines of 0.1mm thickness drawn 0.3mm apart will thicken and fill in to produce one bold line – possibly not the effect intended.

When the illustrations were complete, laser prints were shown to the client,

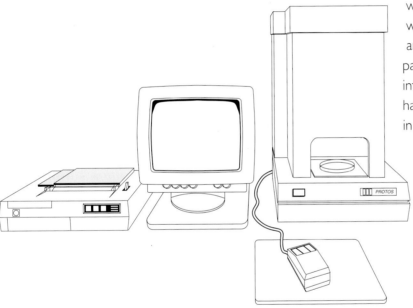

who accepted them. The files were then put onto floppy disk and given to the client. He pasted them – electronically – into his final document which had been written and designed in a page layout program.

The images were successful and I went on to produce illustrations of several further products in the same way.

This figure reveals the perspective lines used for the above image.

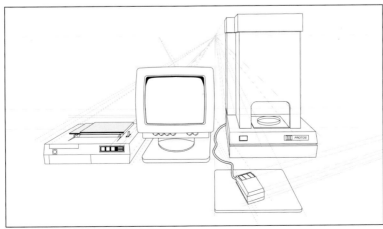

Two-colour collage

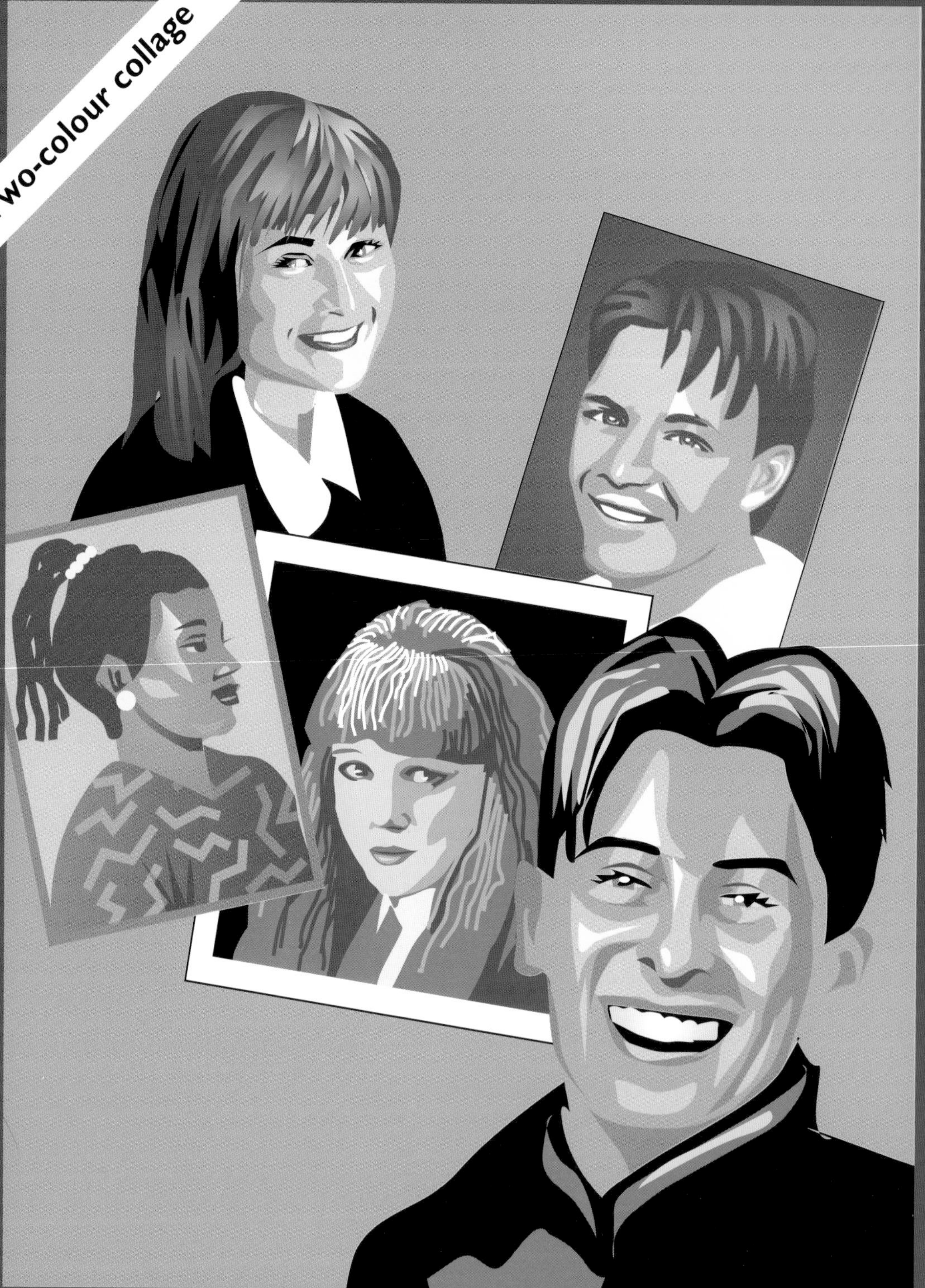

A cover design and image were needed for a workbook entitled *Where next?* This was a publication aimed at teachers counselling young school leavers in jobsearch skills. The text covered subjects such as how to write a CV and interview techniques. The author agreed that the cover should have a very positive, energetic feel to it.

The cover was going to be shown at a much reduced size in publicity material (this book was going to be available by mail order) so it needed to have quite a bold, poster-like quality to withstand reduction.

It was important to show a range of gender and race, and a collage seemed the ideal solution. I bought a selection of teenage magazines as reference and began my search for a variety of portraits. I wanted to emphasize the individuality of each young person, and decided to give each one a different treatment; one in black and white, another in a mixture of two colours, yet another framed in a border and so on. I had two colours available to me and was determined to gain maximum impact from both of them.

1. Purpose?
To make a strong, attractive and positive graphic image.

2. Who is it for?
Teachers advising young school leavers (the contents were designed to be photocopied and handed out).

6. Your particular skills
Producing many different tints and textures in each of the two colours to produce a rich effect.

3. How long will it be seen?
Likely to be a standard text, so possibly a very long lifespan.

5. Budget/Time?
Ten to twelve hours.

4. How will it be reproduced?
In two colours on a smooth board.

I decided that the second colour should be a warm hue, to give good skin tones. Faces portrayed in shades of green or purple can look a little cadaverous! I finally settled on Pantone 185, which I felt was dark enough to give a full range of tints, and yet was pink enough to give the faces quite healthy complexions.

Work started on the figure in the backgound. I decided to use slabs of flat colour in a variety of tints to build up the form of the face.

The hair was built up with a selection of radial tints to give the effect of glossiness.

A tint was dropped into the background. This gave the option of creating areas and highlights in lighter colours, as well as drawing in darker tints.

After working for a considerable time, I began to feel that the colour wasn't working as well as anticipated. Tints of Pantone 185 seemed to have an umpleasant 'bubble-gum' appearance. Perhaps it was worth trying a few other colours? One of the great strengths of the computer is the ease with which colours can be edited. When a basic hue is changed, all the tints made from that hue also change.

Gold was bright and lively, but unsuccessful in that being a naturally light hue it didn't give a sufficient range of tints.

Pantone 174, a brown, gave a wide range of tints. The lighter ones had an attractive sepia quality which would enhance the photographic appearance of the bordered pictures.

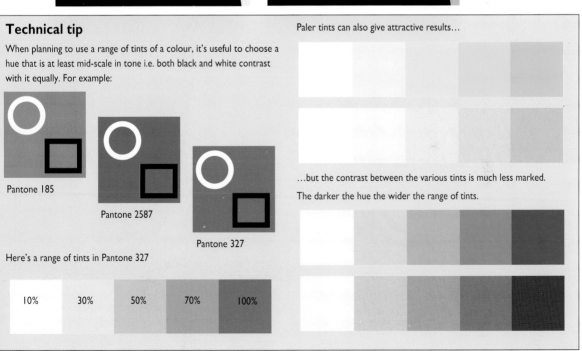

Technical tip

When planning to use a range of tints of a colour, it's useful to choose a hue that is at least mid-scale in tone i.e. both black and white contrast with it equally. For example:

Pantone 185

Pantone 2587

Pantone 327

Here's a range of tints in Pantone 327

10%	30%	50%	70%	100%

Paler tints can also give attractive results…

…but the contrast between the various tints is much less marked.

The darker the hue the wider the range of tints.

This girl's hair, being coarse and curly, suggested another technique to add contrast; I used a range of thick lines in different tints instead of the solid patches used on the other portraits.

When drawing faces it is surprising how much vitality can be added by the careful use of highlights. Contrast the two examples here. The addition of a few simple light patches greatly increases the three-dimensional quality.

Let's examine one of the images step-by-step.

The main areas were drawn in. A subtle radial tint worked well on the basic area of the face.

This started the modelling process which was then enhanced with the addition of some highlights. Hair and jewellery details were added.

The girl's sweater was drawn and shaded with a graduated tint.

The patterning was added in the form of zig zag lines in a pale tint.

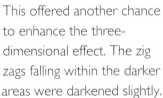

This offered another chance to enhance the three-dimensional effect. The zig zags falling within the darker areas were darkened slightly. The zig zags extending beyond the edges are clipped off, and the girl is finished.

The final composite image had the intended effect. It was quite bold, having a poster-style quality. The title, author's name and publisher's logo fitted into the spaces left for them top right and bottom left.

GAMES & SPORTS

INTERESTED ORGANISATIONS

MAJOR SPECTATOR SPORTS

MOVEMENT & DANCE

OUTDOOR PURSUITS

WATER RECREATION

The briefing for this series of images was very loose. The client was a printer who was handling the design, typesetting and printing of an annual booklet for the Central Council of Physical Recreation. We had all worked together on several previous projects and had built up a good understanding of what was expected of each other. It's always a great pleasure to get to this stage in a relationship with a client. The first commission for a new client is often an anxious time, as neither of you are quite sure of the outcome.

In this case I was dealing with the typesetting, design, illustration and production of the finished artwork as positive film separations. For all these processes to be the responsibility of a single person is a relatively recent development. Not so long ago, typesetters dealt solely with words, and artists solely with pictures. Now the barriers are breaking down; authors and typesetters will sometimes tackle their own simple diagrams and illustrations, and illustrators will sometimes lay out the text around their images. This leads to a much more stimulating challenge for the graphic illustrator.

In this case I was handed a manuscript, told that it was to be an A5 booklet, full colour throughout, and that six illustrations of the main themes were required to liven it up as no other pictures were available. There was no list of these themes provided, so I had to read through the text to find them. They were not immediately obvious, but fortunately I must have chosen the right ones as no-one queried my selection!

1. Purpose?
Purely decorative.

2. Who is it for?
Anyone involved in the organization of sporting clubs and activities.

6. Your particular skills
Making a rich, graphic pattern.

Illustration

3. For how long will it be seen?
Reprinted and redesigned every year, so possible to use a free, semi-abstract style.

5. Budget/Time?
One hour per illustration.

4. How will it be reproduced?
Full colour on good quality paper.

Once the extent of the text had been determined it became apparent that there wasn't a lot of room available for the graphics. I decided to make them almost heraldic, trying to concentrate the meaning of each into a dense graphic image. The illustrations needed to have energy and dynamism, to reflect the sporting topics. This aspect was emphasised by creating a rigid frame and allowing the elements to break out of it. I decided that the colours should be rich rather than bright when selecting a palette of colours.

The six images were planned out in pencil, then the first was produced in its entirety. This was quite time-consuming, so it was decided at this point to present the client with just the one finished illustration, and the rest as pencil roughs. This would give a clear impression of the intended results without heavy expenditure of time – the client had yet to see the ideas, and might reject them.

Fortunately, all the images met with complete approval and work continued on the remaining five illustrations.

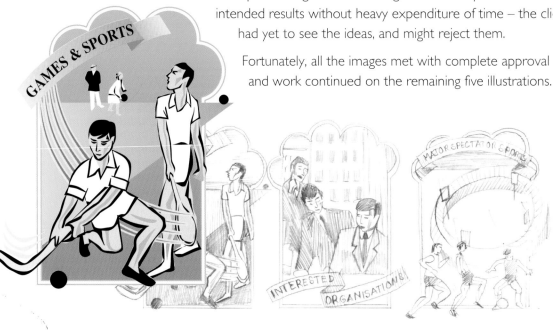

The shapes were mapped out on the background layer in the very basic fashion shown here. Don't be afraid to sketch stick figures in desired poses; they may look a little primitive, but they give a good framework on which to hang the flesh and clothing.

I wanted the banners to have the effect of engraved brass, and used graduated and radial tints to blend the range of bronzes originated for the basic palette of colours.

The final illustrations met with approval, and added a little visual excitement to the publication when scattered throughout the text. They were particularly successful on the title page where they were reduced to the size of postage stamps and arranged in a decorative band.

Technical tip

Parallel lines – so difficult to achieve using traditional techniques – are easy to produce with the computer. In fact, the lines are not drawn parallel to each other, but lines of different weights and colours are overlaid directly on top of each other:

Draw a line…

… then duplicate it to produce another identical line on top. Make this new line thinner, and change the colour to that of the background…

This same technique can be used to create any number of parallel lines:

The finished product

We have dealt with the various decisions which have to be made before work can begin, and the different processes which can make the task easier and more accurate. Now we have reached the final stages. Your creative work is complete. The client has approved the laser print of your illustration. What happens next?

First of all, make sure you have backed-up your illustration in a suitable way. If the illustration is important, with a strong likelihood of being used again in the future, it's worth making two back-up copies. I make one on a removable disk drive, and another one on a series of floppy disks. It is advisable to make the copies using different storage methods, so that the sudden failure of part of your hardware doesn't jeopardise your project.

Next, your work needs to be given to the client or printer. This is usually done by copying the files from your hard disk to a floppy disk, but it's possible to send the files through the telephone lines to their destination, via a modem.

Having still only seen a laser print, both you and your client cannot be totally sure what the image will finally look like. A 'proof' is needed. This is a word used so frequently for laser prints or photocopies produced for checking that we forget what it means: 'proof' that your work will create the desired printed result!

There are a variety of proofing processes. For black and white printing a laser print is usually sufficient. Two-, three- and four-colour images demand more sophisticated methods.

The colour laser print is the most economical at present. It produces a very adequate impression of the finished image, and the colours are very accurate.

For real proof that your four-colour illustration will reproduce, a photographic print (often referred to as a Matchprint or Cromalin by printers) is essential. The four positive film separations are outputted from the information on your floppy disk. These films will ultimately be used to make the printing plates, but can first be used, with light sensitive paper and chemicals, to produce this type of proof. A Matchprint or Cromalin will give you real proof that your separations will print. If there is going to be any screen clash it will show up. If one of the films has stretched (very rare, but possible) to give faulty registration, you will see it. This can be of great value in the unhappy event of a dispute with the printer; you have irrefutable evidence that the films you supplied would print to the required standard. The main drawback of photographic proofs is the expense. The proof itself may seem moderately priced, but don't forget that you will already have gone to the expense of producing the separations. A second potential disadvantage is in the precise, intense, glossy quality of the proof. The inks of the printed image never quite match up to this brilliance, and the result can be quite a disappointment for you and your client!

A new technique has recently become available which falls half way between the colour copy and the photographic print. This is a photographic print which is produced directly from disk. This has the advantage of not requiring the positive films to be produced first, and therefore sidesteps that expense. However, the proof comprises a continuous tone, and is therefore not a true representation of the four-colour process. This means that problems such as screen clash and misregister will not show up, and therefore it cannot give

you or your client actual proof that your set of films will work on the printing press. The best use is probably for very high quality visuals rather than as a proofing technique in its own right.

Even further along the production process we have 'wet proofs'. At this point the films have been checked, the final (one hopes) plates made and sent to a specialist proofing house. Here, under very controlled conditions of temperature and humidity, a small number of proofs are carefully made. This is the genuine printed image, and the last possible stage when errors can be corrected before the main print run.

It can be worth chasing your client for finished, printed examples of your work. They are not always automatically sent out to everyone who has worked on them, but usually a client is only too pleased to give you copies. On the rare occasions where you have worked on something with a very high unit cost – an encyclopedia for instance – it may not be possible to have a copy for your folio. It's still worth making sure that you see the finished, printed item, even if you only have chance to examine it in your client's office. Only by carefully analyzing your illustrations in print can you build up a good picture of what works and what doesn't, and where it works best.

The satisfaction of illustration as a career comes from working within the restrictions imposed by the client's tastes and budget, the printing process and the paper surface, the potential viewer and his or her interests, and your own strengths and weaknesses to produce an image which is dynamic, elegant and succinct. Often it isn't easy, but ultimately it can be very rewarding.

Glossary

Bureau

The most commonly-used term for a company specializing in the output of film and bromide from disk. They may also offer many other services, such as design, keying-in, proof-reading and colour proofing. This is a new niche created by new technology, and combines many of the traditional functions of the typesetter and repro house.

Clip art library

The term for computer-generated images on software which can be purchased and used, free of copyright. As a professional illustrator you probably won't find much use for this – you'll be creating your own images. One possible exception is a good selection of maps; they save you time which can then be spent on the more creative aspects of your work.

Continuous tone

A photograph is an example of this. Close examination with a magnifying glass will reveal that tones blend smoothly together, with no hard edges or half-tone dots. It is not possible to print a true continuous tone lithographically; it must be reduced to small solid areas, such as cross-hatching or the dots of half-tone screening.

EPS

This stands for Encapsulated PostScript and is the form in which computer illustrations can be stored and used in other programs. A designer incorporating your work into a document need not have the same graphics program as you to use your image in this form. It is also a security measure; the EPS can be scaled, rotated and flipped, but alterations cannot be made to the elements of which it is composed.

Floppy disk

A disk of magnetic material enclosed in a slim, plastic case, either 3½" or 5¼" in diameter. Floppy disks are very durable and can withstand a considerable amount of ill-treatment, as long as the magnetic storage material isn't exposed and damaged. They are perfect for sending information through the post, and the most common method of sending work to the bureau for output. They are also a very reliable and economical form of back-up. Their limiting factor is the relatively small amount of information they can hold. A complex document or illustration may demand something of greater capacity (see **removable drive, optical storage**).

Half-tone screen

A pattern of small solid areas, usually dots, of different frequencies to give and illusion of a tint of a colour.

Light box

A box with a semi-transparent top, illuminated from within. Although less necessary in the computer age than formerly, this is still a very useful piece of equipment for the artist or designer. Photographic transparencies can be easily viewed when back-lit by a light box, and positive film separations checked. The most useful light box for the artist or designer has a parallel motion attached, and doubles up as a drawing board.

Moiré

An interference pattern caused by the misalignment of screens. The dot patterns must be at very precise angles to each other, and if one or more screens are incorrectly angled a coloured area of the print can have a lumpy, mottled or woven appearance. This is also called **screen-clash**.

Optical storage

A piece of hardware to be attached to your computer which has enormous data storage capacity. As with the removable drive, the cartridges can be changed at will and it's possible to build up a library of them as necessary. One possible drawback – the failure of a cartridge could result in enormous loss of data!

Overlay

A sheet of transparent or semi-opaque material attached to base artwork, on which either notes to the printer are written or further artwork is created for a second colour to be overprinted. The most usual materials are tracing paper, layout paper or plastic draughting film. The practice is rapidly becoming less commonplace as the production of final separations is coming within easy reach of the designer.

Pantone Matching System (PMS)

A world-wide system of matching colours, used by both designers and printers. The purchase of a swatch book of colours for reference is recommended. This shows the colour on both coated and uncoated paper. Don't forget that varnishing or laminating also alters colours; wetting a small area with water will give a good representation of this.

PICT

A format for storing scanned pictures.

Plate

Today most work is printed by offset lithography, the principle of which is the mutual repulsion of grease and water. The plate is made of aluminium, plastic or paper, on which the image is imprinted in a greasy substance. It is then made wet with water and ink only adheres to the greasy image. At this point the image is printed onto a rubber surface which prints onto the paper – hence offset lithography.

As an illustrator, one doesn't have to be too familiar with plates and platemaking techniques, but in the computer age your responsibility does extend right up to the positive and negative films which are directly used to transfer the image to the plate.

Positive film separations

When the illustration is complete, the file is taken from the computer (on floppy disk or removable cartridge, via modem, or directly through a cable link) and processed by further hardware to produce either a black and white print (bromide), or positive or negative films. For colour illustration, two-, three-, four- or more such films are output, each film containing the information for each separate colour to be printed. Negative films lend themselves to black and white publications; positive films are easier and more effective for colour work.

Process colours

These are the four coloured inks used in most full-colour printing. They are often referred to – especially on the computer – as CMYK, standing for Cyan, Magenta, Yellow and Black (K is used instead of B for black to avoid confusion with blue). Dots of varying sizes and frequencies are overprinted to produce an illusion of a continuous tone, full-colour image.

Registration marks

Marks occuring on every separation for colour printing which ensure correct registration. They most commonly consist of a cross and circle, printed outside the trim area. Many computer programs create them automatically, but they can be added individually. Crop marks can also act as registration marks for simple artwork, but their main function is to ensure accurate trimming at the printers.

Removable drive

A piece of hardware for data storage which can be attached to your computer and into which can be inserted interchangeable cartridges. These can store large amounts of information, and the cartridges can be stored on a shelf, taking up very little space. They are also a reasonably secure method of sending larger documents to the bureau for output

Repro house

A company specializing in the production of separated films, tint-laying, scanning of photographs, creation of half-tones, plate-making and proofing by means of photographic colour prints. This part of the printing industry has undergone a period of violent change with the advent of desktop publishing. Many of the skills it has traditionally offered have become obsolete as the production of ready-for-platemaking separations have come under the control of the artist. Many have had to change their functions and become DTP bureaux, offering digital scanning and output facilities.

Scanner

There are many varieties of scanner available, and they are becoming cheaper, faster and more accurate at an ever-increasing rate. The first problem encountered when

using the computer as an illustration tool is how to transfer your rough sketch or tracing onto the screen, and even the most rudimentary scanner can help in this. A very advanced desktop scanner can scan images to printable quality. The repro house or bureau is likely to be the type of organization able to afford the very advanced scanners, giving superb quality. At present the reasonable prices charged for their services make it preferable to buy in top quality colour scanning when necessary.

Screen clash

See **moiré**

Silk screen

This is an advanced development of stencilling. The stencil can be produced by hand or photographically. The finely woven screen (made of man-made fibres these days — not silk) is used to support the stencil, and the ink is pushed through the fine mesh with a rubber 'squeegee'. Silk-screen is used mostly in the manufacture of signs and it's not likely as an illustrator that you will encounter it very often. When creating images for this process, remember to use a fairly bold line, and beware of fine tints (the screen of these can clash with the silk-screen itself, creating a moiré effect).

Special

A fifth printing of a colour over and above the four process colours. This can be a varnish (see **Spot varnish**) or a Pantone colour.

Spot varnish

A fifth printing with a clear, glossy varnish over selected areas of the image. The whole area can be varnished to create a glossy, wipe-clean surface. This also deepens and enriches the colours. The same effect can be achieved by laminating.

Still video camera

A camera the size of a traditional camera which holds a floppy disk instead of film and takes digital pictures. This can be linked to a VCR to display the images on the domestic TV screen, or directly to a computer for use in the same way as scanned images.

TIFF

Stands for Tag Image File Format, and is a format for storing scanned pictures (see also EPS and PICT).

Bibliography

Drawing techniques and inspiration
Gordon, Louise, *The figure in action*, (B. T. Batsford, 1990)

Lewis, Brian, *An introduction to illustration*, (Apple Press, 1987)

Simpson, Ian (Editor), *The new guide to illustration*, (Phaidon, 1990)

White, Gwen, *Perspective*, (B. T. Batsford, 1989)

Printing Techniques
Braham, Bert, *The graphic arts studio manual*, (Collins Sons & Co Ltd., 1986)

Information Transfer, *The print book*, (National Extension College, 1985)

Laing, John (Editor), *Do-it-yourself graphic design*, (Ebury Press, 1984)

Mc Cann, Richard, *Graphics handbook,* (Health Education Council, 1986)

Business skills for the illustrator
Goslett, Dorothy, *The professional practice of design*, (B. T. Batsford, Third Edition, Reprinted 1993)

Illustration for a book cover: Technical writing

Index